ON THE FREEDOM
OF THE WILL

De Libero Arbitrio Voluntatis

By SAINT AUGUSTINE

Translated by
CARROLL MASON SPARROW

On the Freedom of the Will
By Saint Augustine
Translated by Carroll Mason Sparrow

Print ISBN 13: 978-1-4209-7194-1

This edition copyright © 2020. Digireads.com Publishing.

Cover Image: a detail of "The Vision of Saint Augustine", by Vittore Carpaccio, c. 16th century / Luisa Ricciarini / Bridgeman Images.

Please visit *www.digireads.com*

CONTENTS

BOOK ONE

In which, the question being raised: whence comes evil?—it is explained what evildoing is; then it is shown that the evil deeds of men proceed from the free choice of the will, since the mind is in no way compelled to follow the lust that holds sway in every evil act.

BOOK TWO

Wherein, a difficulty having arisen from the fact that the freedom of
the will wherewith we sin is given by God, these three questions are
studied: first, by what reasoning is it clear that God exists; second,
whether all goods are from God; third, whether free will is to be
accounted a good.

BOOK THREE

Wherein it is asked whence arises that movement by which the will is turned away from immutable good. Do God's foreknowledge of the sins of men, and the freedom of men themselves to sin conflict with one another? It is presently shown that the Creator is nowise at fault for what so happens by necessity in the creature that it is done by the will of sinners; and that for the prolonging and punishment of creatures who are liable to sin God is wholy to be praised. The argument then leading to the subject of original sin, it is made clear wherefore it continues not at all unjustly in the descendants of Adam, and that sinners undeservingly plead this as an excuse. Finally, some difficulties connected with this are unraveled.

Contents

FOREWORD

THIS translation of St. Augustine's *De libero arbitrio voluntatis* is the work of the late Carroll Mason Sparrow. The translation was accomplished during the last years of his life, probably during the four years preceding his death in 1941. It is the last manifestation of the extraordinarily varied interests of the translator, a physicist by training and profession, but increasingly interested in the history of ideas, in the philosophy of science, and in theology.

It was deemed advisable to have the translation checked against the original. In undertaking this task the reviser has made every effort to preserve the character and quality of the translation as left by Professor Sparrow. He is keenly aware that any translation is vulnerable to criticism. In many instances the reviser would have adopted an approach and a phraseology different from that of Professor Sparrow. But he regarded the task of revision as a limited one, and accordingly has made only such changes as were deemed necessary for clear exposition of the original. The translation presented herewith is in every essential as it was left by the translator.

The changes effected by the reviser fall into several groups. Many were corrections of obviously typographical errors. Some changes were of a grammatical nature. There were cases in which the translator neglected, in the interests of clarity and smoothness of translation, the clausal balance and structure so favored by Patristic authors. The reviser felt that indications in the text of each and every one of these changes would interrupt continuity of thought and expression. The indications of changes have accordingly been kept to a minimum. Here and there were omissions, due, it appears, to the fact that the translator relied primarily upon the Tourscher Latin text (1937) which does not include some passages given in the more complete text of Migne (1841). The reviser has supplied a translation of the omitted texts, and these passages are indicated by inclosure in brackets.

All footnotes, except those signed "M", are Professor Sparrow's. All starred footnotes that refer to passages in the Vulgate are taken from Tourscher's text. Here and there, in the reviser's judgment, Professor Sparrow's translation departs from the thought development of the original. In such cases the reviser has provided alternative renderings, and these have been placed as footnotes marked by the initial "M".

At the request of the publishers, Professor R. P. McKeon made a careful examination of the translation. The reviser has profited by a study of his incisive and scholarly criticisms, and makes cordial acknowledgment of his obligation. It should be added that Professor Sparrow availed himself of Professor McKeon's admirable translation of the section of Book II, chapters I-XVIII, as published in the first volume of his Selections from Medieval Philosophers, Charles Scribner's Sons, 1929, and left indications in the manuscript of his intention to make due acknowledgment of the fact.

The reviser's personal thanks are due also to Mr. Jack Preston Dalton, of the Staff of the Alderman Memorial Library in the University of Virginia, for his valuable assistance in checking the manuscript against the original.

Cordial appreciation is also due to Professor Albert G. A. Balz, who has had responsibility for planning the publication of manuscripts left by Professor Sparrow. A collection of essays, for which this translation of Augustine may be regarded as a companion volume, has appeared under the title, *Voyages and Cargoes*.

WALTER A. MONTGOMERY,
Emeritus Professor of Latin,
The University of Virginia.

ON THE FREEDOM OF THE WILL

ON THE FREEDOM OF THE WILL

BOOK ONE

IN WHICH, THE QUESTION BEING RAISED: WHENCE COMES EVIL?
—IT IS EXPLAINED WHAT EVILDOING IS; THEN IT IS SHOWN THAT
THE EVIL DEEDS OF MEN PROCEED FROM THE FREE CHOICE
OF THE WILL, SINCE THE MIND IS IN NO WAY COMPELLED TO
FOLLOW THE LUST THAT HOLDS SWAY IN EVERY EVIL ACT.

CHAPTER I

Whether God is the author of any evil.

1. *Evodius.* Tell me, pray, whether God is not the author of evil?

Augustine. I will tell you, if you will make clear what kind of evil you mean. For we are wont to speak of evil in two senses: one, when we say that someone has done evil; another, when we say that he has suffered some evil.

E. I want to know about both.

A. But if you know or believe that God is good—and to think otherwise is impious—He does no evil. Again, if we acknowledge God to be just—which it were blasphemy to deny—as He rewards the good, so He metes out punishments to the wickèd, which punishments are assuredly evil for those who suffer them. Wherefore, if no one is punished unjustly —which we are bound to believe, since we believe the world is ruled by divine providence—God is in no way the author of that first kind of evil; but of the second kind He is the author.

E. Is there then another author of that evil of which God is not the author?

A. Surely—for it could not be done but by some author. But if you ask who he may be, that cannot be said; for it is no one somebody, but each wicked man is the author of his own evil deeds. If that is not clear, think of what we just said:

evil deeds are avenged by God's justice. But they could not
be avenged justly unless they were done willingly.

2. *E.* I do not know whether one can sin, unless he has learned
to sin. But if this be true, who, I ask, is he from whom we
have learned it?

A. Do you think that education is a good thing?

E. Who would dare to say that education is bad?

A. What if it be neither a good nor a bad thing?

E. I think it is a good thing.

A. Very well: so long at least as it imparts or arouses
knowledge. Nor does one learn anything without being edu-
cated. Or do you not agree?

E. I think that only good things are learned by education.

A. But look you then, in that case we cannot learn evil
things; for the very word education (*disciplina*) means learning (*discendo*).*

E. How then do men commit evil deeds, if they do not learn
how?

A. Perhaps it is because they turn away and are separated
from education, that is, from learning. But whether it be this
or something else, this much is surely obvious: since education
is a good thing; and education (*disciplina*) gets its name
from the act of learning (*discendo*)*, it is not at all possible
to learn evil things. For if they are learned, they are contained in a discipline, and so the discipline will not be a
good thing. But it is good, as you yourself admit. Therefore
evil things are not learned, and we seek in vain for him from
whom we learn to do ill; or if they are learned we learn to
avoid them, not to do them. Thus to do evil can only be to
depart from the way of learning.

3. *E.* I am strongly of the opinion that there are two kinds of
education: one by which we learn to do well, and another by

---

*The continual interplay between *disciplina* and *discere* is impossible to
translate.

which we learn to do ill. But while you were asking whether education was good, my mind was so taken up by love of the good, that I was looking only at the education for well-doing; so I said it was good. But now I am reminded that there is another, which I affirm to be evil beyond doubt; and it is of this that I would know the author.

A. You think, at any rate, that understanding is only good?

E. That, I think, is so obviously good that I cannot see what in man can be more excellent; and I would never say that any sort of understanding can be bad.

A. How then, if one is taught, but does not understand; would you say that he had learned anything?

E. By no means.

A. If therefore all understanding is good, and he who understands nothing learns nothing, then everyone who learns does well. Whoever, therefore, seeks the author through whom we learn anything, seeks surely the author through whom we do well. So stop trying to discover some wicked teacher or other; for if he is wicked he is not a teacher, and if he is a teacher he is not wicked.

CHAPTER II

Before inquiring into the origin of evil, it must be asked what we should believe concerning God.

4. *E.* Since you force me to acknowledge that we do not learn to do evil, go on now, and tell me why we do it.

A. You raise a question with which I wrestled mightily as a young man, and which drove me, wearied, into the company of heretics and cast me down. So hurt was I by that fall, and so smothered in a rubbish-heap of idle talk, that if my love of finding the truth had not won for me divine aid, I should never have come out to draw my first free breath of inquiry. And since I had to struggle hard to be rid of that problem, I will retrace with you the path by which I escaped. For God will be with us, and He will give us understanding of that which we believe. For we are well assured that we are keeping to the course prescribed by the Prophet who said: *Except ye believe, ye shall not understand.** We believe moreover that all things that are are from the one God, [and yet that God is not the author of sins]. But the mind is troubled by the problem: If sins come from souls which God has created, and those souls are from God, how comes it that sins are not, at a slight remove, to be thrown back upon God?

5. *E.* Now you have put clearly what I have been racking my brain to think out, and what drove and drew me to this questioning.

A. Be of stout heart, and believe what you believe. For nothing is better worth believing, even if the reason be hid from us. For in very truth, to hold God supreme is the beginning of piety. Nor does anyone hold Him supreme who does not believe Him almighty and least unchanging; creator also of all things good, whose excellence He himself transcends; most just ruler also of all that He has made, and made without help of any nature—as if, forsooth, He were not self-sufficing. Whence it follows that He made all things from nothing. From His own substance, however, He did not create; but begot that which to Him is equal, whom we call the only Son of God, but whom when we try to speak more clearly we call the Power of God, and the Wisdom of God; through whom He made all those things that are made from nothing. So much being settled, let us strive in this manner toward an understanding of the matter about which you ask.

CHAPTER III

The nature of evil is from lust.

6.   You ask, to be sure, why we do evil. But first we must discuss what evil-doing is; so let me have your views on this point. Or, if you cannot state the whole matter in a few words, give me your view by enumerating some particular evil deeds.

---

*Isaiah VII, 9; In the Vulgate, *permanebitis* for *intelligetis.*

E. Adultery, and murder, and blasphemy; not to mention the others, which even could I remember them all would take too long to name. Who is there who would not deem these evil?
A. Tell me then, first, why you think adultery wrong. Is it wrong because the law forbids it?
E. Surely no. It is not wrong because the law forbids it; rather is it forbidden because it is wrong.
A. How if someone were to take issue with us, magnifying the delights of adultery, and wanting to know why we think it evil and deserving of condemnation. Do you think that those who want not only to believe, but to understand, must fall back on the law for a reason? For I too believe with you, and steadfastly, and proclaim it as worthy of belief by all peoples and races, that adultery is wrong. But we are now endeavoring to hold in the secure grasp of understanding what we have received by faith. So give the matter your best thought, and tell me for what reason you know adultery to be wrong.
E. I know it to be wrong because I would be unwilling to suffer it in my own wife. But whoever does to another what he would not want done to himself, surely does wrong.
A. What if someone finds a perverted pleasure in offering his wife to another, and willingly allows her to be debauched by him, desiring in turn to have the same license with the wife of the other man? Does such a wrong seem to you to do no wrong?
E. Nay, he does all manner of wrong.
A. But by your rule he offends not; for he does nothing that he would be unwilling to have done to him. So you must look for something else to prove that adultery is wrong.
E. It seems wrong to me because I have often seen men condemned for the crime.
A. What, have you not often seen men condemned for doing right? Not to send you to other books, review your history; that very history which by its divine authority excels all other. See how badly we must think of the Apostles and all the

Martyrs, if we are going to take condemnation as sure proof of guilt; since they were all adjudged worthy of condemnation on what they themselves confessed. If, therefore, whatever is condemned is wrong, it was at that time wrong to believe in Christ, and to confess the Christian faith; but if not everything that is condemned is bad, try to find some other reason for saying that adultery is wrong.

E. I find naught wherewith to answer you.

8. A. Is it not perhaps the concupiscence that is the evil thing in adultery, and that you are having difficulty because you are looking for evil in the act itself, which can be seen? For that the concupiscence is the evil thing in adultery can be seen from this: if a man had not the opportunity for lying with another's wife, but if it were none the less somehow evident that he wanted to, and would do so if given the occasion, he is no less a criminal than if he were taken in the very act.

E. Nothing is more altogether evident; and now I see that there is no need for a long discourse to convince me about murder and blasphemy, and any sins whatsoever. For it is now clear that it is the sinful desire, and nothing else, that holds first place in every kind of evil-doing.

CHAPTER IV

An objection concerning murder committed through fear. What a culpable desire is.

9. A. You know, do you not, that this concupiscence is also called by another name, covetousness?

E. I know.

A. Well now, do you think there is no difference between covetousness and fear, or is there a difference?

E. Nay indeed, I think there is a wide gulf between them.

A. I imagine you think so because covetousness seeks, while fear flees from its object.

E. Exactly.

A. Suppose now that someone, not because he coveted anything, but out of fear lest some evil should befall him, should kill a man. Would he be a murderer?

E. He would, surely. But the deed is not in this case free from the sway of covetousness; for he who for fear kills a man, at any rate covets a life free from fear.

A. And do you reckon it a slight good to live free of fear?

E. It is a great good. But it can in no wise come to that murderer through his act.

A. I am not asking what can come to him, but what he covets. For surely he covets a good thing who covets a life free from fear; hence we may not blame the coveting except by blaming all lovers of the good. Thus we are forced to admit that there may be a murder in which the domination of evil desire cannot be found; and it will not be true that in all sins it is the domination of concupiscence that makes them evil: either that, or there will be some murders that cannot be sins.

E. If murder means killing a man, then it can sometimes happen without sin; for the soldier kills an enemy, and the judge or his deputy kills a criminal. Also, if a javelin goes wild from a careless hand against the thrower's will. None of these seem to me to sin when they kill a man.

A. I agree with you; but these are not wont to be called murderers. So answer this: suppose a man kills a master from whom he fears severe punishment. Would you count him among those who so kill men as not to deserve the name of murderer?

E. That seems to me an entirely different case; for those others acted either in obedience to the law, or not against the law. But no law approves the act of this man.

10. *A.* You keep coming back to authority. But you should remember that we took up this matter in order to understand what we take on trust. We take the laws on trust; and so we must try to understand, if we can, whether the law that punishes this deed may not punish it wrongly.

E. By no means does it punish wrongly one who willingly and knowingly kills his master. None of those others did that.

A. Come now, do you remember saying a little while ago, that in every evil deed an evil desire holds sway, and that it is because of that desire that the deed is evil?

E. To be sure I remember.

A. And did you not also grant that he who desires to live without fear has not an evil desire?

E. I remember that too.

A. Since therefore the master is slain by the slave so desiring, he is not slain by reason of a culpable desire. Wherefore we have not yet found why his deed is wrong. For we have agreed that all evil deeds are evil only because of concupiscence. They are done from lust, that is, from blame worthy desire.

E. It looks now as if he were wrongly condemned: a thing I certainly would not dare to say if I had anything else left to say.

A. But have you not persuaded yourself that so great a crime should go unpunished because you failed to consider that the slave desired to be free of his master in order to satisfy his own evil desires. For to live without fear is not only the desire of good men, but of all wicked men as well. But with this difference: that the good men seek this end by turning their affections away from those things which cannot be held without the danger of losing them; whereas the wicked, in order that they may rest secure in their enjoyment of such things, attempt to remove obstacles, and so pursue a life of misdeed and crime—a life that better deserves the name of death.

E. I am getting back my senses; and I am overjoyed to see clearly just what is that culpable desire that is called concupiscence. This now stands out as the love of those things which a man can lose against his will.

CHAPTER V

Another objection, concerning the killing, permitted by human laws, of one who offers violence.

11.   So now let us inquire, if you will, whether concupiscence rules also in acts of sacrilege, which for the most part seem to be committed through superstition.

A. Do not go too fast. It seems to me that we should first discuss whether an attacking enemy, or an ambushed assassin, may without concupiscence be killed to protect life, or liberty, or honor.

E. How can I deem them without concupiscence, since they contend for those things which they may lose against their will; or if they can prevent loss, why go so far as to kill for their sake?

A. Then the law is not just that gives the wayfarer the right to kill a robber to save his own life, or that permits anyone, man or woman, to kill an attacking ravisher before he can accomplish his purpose? The law moreover commands the soldier to kill the enemy; if he stays his hand he is punished by the emperor. Shall we venture to say that such laws are unjust, or that they are indeed not laws at all? For I think that a law that is not just is no law.

12. *E.* I see that the law is indeed safe enough from such a charge; for the law permits the people that it governs to commit lesser wrongs to prevent the commission of greater. For the death of one who lies in wait to kill another is a much slighter thing than that of one who would merely save his own life. And it is a far worse thing to force humiliation on a man than that the ravisher be killed by his intended victim. As for the soldier, in killing his enemy he is the servant of the law, and hence merely does his duty without any evil desire. Moreover the law itself, being made for the protection of the people, cannot be accused of concupiscence. For he who made the law, if he made it by God's command—that is to say following the dictates of eternal justice—could do so

without any concupiscence whatever; but even if he decreed it because of some evil desire, it does not follow that the law is necessarily tainted with concupiscence, because a good law may be made even by one who is himself not good. Thus, for example, if one possessed of tyrannical power takes a bribe from some interested person to decree that no one may take a woman by force, even for marriage; the fact that it was made by a corrupt and unjust man does not make it a bad law. Therefore that law which to preserve the state commands that the violence of an enemy be repelled with like violence, may be obeyed without concupiscence. And the same may be said of all officials who by rank and station are subject to any authority. But I do not see how these men, though blameless under the law, can be altogether blameless; for the law does not compel them to kill, but leaves it in their power. And so they are left free not to kill anyone for those things which they can lose against their will, and which therefore they ought not to love. As for the life of the soul, it is at least doubtful whether it can be taken away by killing the body. But if it can be taken, it is worthless; if not, there is naught to fear. As to chastity, who indeed doubts that it is in the soul, for chastity is a virtue. Hence it cannot be taken away by the violence of the ravisher. Whatever, therefore, he who is killed was going to take from us is not in our control, so that I do not understand in what sense it can be called ours. Wherefore, while I do not condemn the law that permits such people to be killed, I do not see how to defend those who kill them.

13. *A.* Much less can I see why you seek a defense for men whom no law holds guilty.

E. No law, perhaps, if you mean those public laws which men may read. But I know not whether they are not bound by some higher unwritten law, if all things are ruled by divine providence. For how are they free of sin before Providence, who for things that they should despise stain their hands with human blood? Wherefore it seems to me that the law that is written for governing the people, rightly permits these things, and that divine providence avenges them. For the law of the people undertakes to uphold those things that suffice to keep the peace among ignorant men, so far as they can be controlled by men. But those other sins have other fitting penalties, from which I think wisdom alone can free us.

A. I commend and approve this distinction of yours. Though incomplete and somewhat imperfect, it is none the less aimed with faith at things sublime. For you see that the law that is made for the government of the states allows to go unpunished many things that yet are avenged by divine providence. And this is right; nor because it does not do everything should we find fault with what it does.

CHAPTER VI

The eternal law rules over human laws. The concept of eternal law.

14.   But let us try to see, if you will, how far misdeeds are to be punished by the law that governs peoples in this life; and hence what is left for divine providence to punish more inevitably in its own way.

E. I should like to, if only we can reach the bounds of so great a matter; for to me it seems limitless.

A. Truly: but put your mind to it, and trusting in piety set out on the path of reason. For there is nothing so obscure, or so difficult, that it may not with God's help be set in clearest light. And so, relying on Him, and praying to Him for help, let us begin our quest. First, then, tell me whether the law that is promulgated in written form is helpful to men living this life.

E. Clearly so; for states and peoples are composed of such men.

A. Now are men and peoples things of the kind that do not perish or change and are altogether eternal, or are they changeable and subject to circumstances?

E. Who can doubt that they are changeable and a prey to time?

A. Therefore if a people be sober and well-disposed, jealous guardians of the common interest, with everyone putting his private interests below the public good; is not that law made rightly by which the people themselves are allowed to set up magistrates of their own choice, through whom their affairs, that is to say the public affairs, are administered?

E. Surely so.

A. If again this same people, becoming gradually depraved, sets private interest above the common good, and holding votes for sale, and corrupted by ambitious men, hands over its government to unprincipled men and criminals, would it not likewise be right if there then arose some honest man of great ability, who took away from this same people the right to confer honors, and put them again under the rule of a few honest men, or even of one?

E. That too would be right.

A. Since therefore these two laws seem to be opposed to each other, the one giving the people the right to confer honors, and the other taking that right away; and since this second law is so made that under no circumstances can both laws exist in the same state: shall we say that one of them is unjust, and should never have been made?

E. By no means.

A. Let us therefore call that law temporal, if you will, which however just it may be, may none the less justly be changed with the course of time.

E. Agreed.

15. *A.* But how now of that law which we call supreme reason, which must always be obeyed, and by which wicked men earn a wretched life, and good men a happy one; and according to which moreover that law that we call temporal is rightly made and rightly changed? Could anyone who understands that law not think it immutable and eternal? Or can it at any time be unjust that the wicked be unhappy, and the good

happy; or that a decent and sober people should set up their own magistrates, but that a dissolute people should lack that power?

E. I see that that law is eternal and immutable.

A. I judge that you see also that in that temporal law there is nothing just or legitimate but what men have derived from the eternal law. For if the people may at one time justly confer honors, and at another time, on the contrary, justly not confer them; this is drawn from that eternal principle, by which it is just that a sober people should confer honors, and a fickle people not. Do you agree?

E. I agree.

A. To put in a few words, as best I may, this notion of eternal law that is impressed on our minds: *It is that law by which it is just that all things be most perfectly ordered.* If you have any objection, speak out.

E. When you say true things I have nothing to say against them.

A. Since therefore there is this one law, by which all those temporal laws for governing men are changed, can it itself be changed in any way?

E. I see clearly that this can nowise be; nor could any force, any chance, any catastrophe, ever bring it to pass that it should not be just that all things should be most perfectly ordered.

CHAPTER VII

It is to be inquired how, according to the eternal law, man is most perfectly ordered. To this end it is shown that to know is better than to live.

16. *A.* And now let us see how man is within himself most perfectly ordered. For nations are composed of men united under one law, and this law, as we have said, is temporal. Tell me then, whether you are very sure that you are living?

E. What indeed, pray, is more certain than that?

A. Well then, do you know this: that to live is one thing; to know that one lives is another?

E. I know indeed that no one but a living being knows that it lives; but whether every living thing knows that it lives, I cannot say.

A. How I wish that as you believe, so also you knew that the beasts lack reason; our discussion could then pass on quickly from this question. But as you say you do not know, you start me on a long discourse. For the matter is such that in so closely reasoned an argument as I feel this must be, we may not pass it by and go on to the things we wish to establish. So tell me this: we have often seen beasts tamed by men; that is, not only the body but the soul of the beast so subject to man that it obeys his will by a sort of instinct or habit. Do you think that it would ever be possible that any beast, no matter how fierce or huge of body, or even how cunning, would attempt to subjugate a man; though many beasts are able by strength or stealth to destroy his body?

E. I agree that that could never happen.

A. Very well: but tell me then also, since it is obvious that man is easily surpassed by many beasts in strength and other bodily faculties; in what thing does man excel, so that no beast can rule him, while he on the other hand can rule many of them? Is it not that very thing that we call reason or understanding?

E. I can think of nothing else, since the way we surpass the brutes is in the soul, so that if they were soulless I would say that we stood above them in having souls. But they have souls; so what better name can I give it than reason? For the lack of it in their souls makes them subject to us; its presence in ours makes us their betters: and no one can deem it naught, or a trifle.

A. See how easily, God helping, that is done which men think most difficult. For I confess to you that I thought that this question, which now seems to be settled, would keep us as long as perhaps everything we have talked about since the beginning of this discussion. So now keep this conclusion in mind, so that the subsequent argument may be connected. For I believe you are aware that what we say we know is none other than what we have perceived by reason.

E. So it is.

A. Therefore whoever knows that he lives is not without reason.

E. That follows.

A. But the beasts live, and as has just been said, they are devoid of reason.

E. That is clear.

A. Behold then, now you know what you said you did not know: that not everything that lives knows that it lives; though everything that knows that it lives necessarily lives.

17. *E.* I no longer doubt. Go on then with what you have in mind; for I am sufficiently assured that to live is one thing, and to know that one lives is another.

A. Which then of these two do you think is the more excellent?

E. Why, surely, the awareness of life.

A. Does the awareness of life seem to you to be better than life itself? Or perhaps you mean that a certain higher and truer life consists in that knowledge of it which those only have who understand. For what is understanding but living more clearly and perfectly by the very light of the mind? So that if I mistake not, you have not set above life something other than life, but above life of a sort have placed a better life.

E. You have understood and restated my meaning most excellently—if only knowledge can never be a bad thing.

A. Never, I think, unless by a shift of meaning we speak of experience as knowledge. For experience is not always good; as when we experience punishment. But who can say that knowledge strictly and properly so called, won by reason and understanding, is bad?

E. I agree with that distinction; go on with the argument.

CHAPTER VIII

Reason, by which man is superior to the beasts, should also have the mastery in man himself.

18. *A.* This is what I wish to say: it is this something—call it mind, or spirit, or more rightly both (for we find both in the sacred Scriptures)—by which man is set above the beasts. If this has mastery and rules all else in man, then is he man most perfectly ordered. For we see that we have many things in common not only with animals, but with trees and plants. We see in fact that it is given to trees also to take bodily nutriment, to grow, to beget, to wax strong; and these belong to a very low kind of life. We know moreover that beasts can see and hear, and perceive corporeal things by taste and smell and touch; and generally more keenly than we. Add strength, and power and endurance of limb, and speed and ease of bodily movement; in all of these we are superior to some and equal to others, but by some we are surpassed. Things like these we certainly share with the brutes; for indeed to seek bodily pleasure and to escape harm are the whole business of a beast's life. There are certain other things which seem not to be the lot of beasts, which yet are not the highest things in man himself, such as jesting and laughing; these are indeed human, but are placed low among human attributes by those who judge human nature rightly. Then again the love of praise and glory, the striving for mastery: these, though the beasts have them not, are not desires by which we may be judged better than the beasts. For these desires, when not subject to reason, make men unhappy; but no one would think himself better than another because of his own wretchedness. When reason is master of these emotions therefore, a man is said to be well-ordered. For it cannot be called right order, or even order at all, when better things are subject to worse. Do you agree?

E. It is obvious.

A. When this reason therefore, or this mind, or spirit, is master of the irrational emotions, then that has the mastery in man to which mastery is due by that law which we found to be eternal.

E. I follow and understand.

CHAPTER IX

The distinction between the wise man and the fool is in the mastery or servitude of the mind.

19. A. When, therefore, a man is so disposed and ordered, do you not deem him wise?

E. I know not whom to think wise, if not such a one.

A. I imagine that you know this too: that most men are fools.

E. That too is pretty well established.

A. But if the fool is the opposite of the wise man, since we have found the wise man, you now also see clearly who the fool is.

E. Who cannot see that it is he in whom the mind has not full mastery?

A. What are we to say, then, of a man in this state: that he has no mind, or that though mind is there it is not in control?

E. The latter, rather.

A. I would like much to hear from you by what evidence you would prove that mind is present in a man when it does not exert its authority.

E. I wish you would take care of this part. It is not easy for me to carry all that you are pouring out.

A. At least it is easy for you to remember what we said a little while ago: how animals are tamed by men and obey their rule; which in turn, as the argument showed, men might suffer from them, if man were not in some way superior. But we found no superiority of body; so that since it appeared to be in the soul we could find no name for it except reason. Later we remembered that it is also called mind and spirit. But even if reason and mind be not the same thing, it is surely clear that only mind can use reason. It follows from this that he who has reason cannot be without a mind.

E. I remember well, and will keep it in mind.

A. Well now, do you believe this: that those who rule beasts must be wise men? For I call wise only those whom truth commands to be so called; that is, those who by the reign of the mind have subdued all lust.

E. It is absurd to think that those who go by the name of trainers are like that—not to mention shepherds and ploughmen, or charioteers; to all of whom we see animals subject, and by whose labors the untamed creatures are made obedient.

A. You have then most certain evidence to show that mind can be present and yet not rule. It is surely present; for they do things that could not be done without mind: nevertheless it does not rule; for they are foolish, and we have seen clearly that the rule of the mind belongs only to wise men.

E. It astonishes me how we reached all these conclusions by earlier arguments, and yet I could not think how to answer.

CHAPTER X

The mind is compelled by no one to be the slave of lust.

20.   But let us treat of other matters. For it is now proved that the rule of the human mind is human wisdom, and also that it may not always rule.

A. Do you think that there is any lust stronger than the mind, to which we know dominion over all lusts was given by the eternal law? For I do not at all think so. For it would not be well-ordered that weaker things should rule over stronger. Wherefore I think it must be that mind is stronger than concupiscence, since it is right and just that it should rule over it.

E. I too think so.

A. Why then do we hesitate so to prefer every virtue to every vice that virtue, better and nobler, should be steadfast and undefeated?

E. Who would hesitate?

A. Therefore no vicious soul may overcome a soul armed with virtue.

E. Most true.

A. I think then that you will not deny that any soul whatsoever is better and more powerful than any body.

E. No one will deny that who sees, as he easily may, that a living substance is to be preferred to a non-living, and that which gives life is above that which receives it.

A. Much less therefore does a body, whatever its nature, overcome a soul endowed with virtue.

E. That is very evident.

A. What of this then? Can a just soul, and a mind watchful of its own right and rule, drive from its stronghold another mind with equal justice and virtue, and subject that ruling mind to lust?

E. By no means; not only because the two are of equal excellence, but also because the first will become a vicious mind in trying to make the other fall, and for that reason will become weaker.

21. *A.* You understand well. One thing more: tell me, if you can, whether anything seems to you more excellent than a wise and reasonable mind.

E. Nothing but God, I think.

A. That is what I think too. But though we hold this with steadfast faith, to reach an understanding of it is a difficult matter; nor is this the time to take it up, as our whole treatment of the question must be thorough and careful.

CHAPTER XI

*That mind is justly punished, which of its own free will is a
slave to lust.*

For the present it is enough to know that whatever be that
nature, that by right is superior to a mind strong in virtue, it
can nowise be unjust; so that not even that, though it have
the power, will compel the mind to serve lust.

E. Surely there is no one who will not unhesitatingly acknowledge that.

A. Since then whatever is equal or superior to a mind
possessed of virtue, and in control, will not for justice sake
make it the slave of lust, and since whatever is inferior cannot
for weakness do so, as follows from what we have established;
there remains only the conclusion that nothing can make the
mind the companion of lust but its own will and free choice.

E. I can see no other conclusion.

22. *A.* I take it then that you think it just to pay penalties for so
great a sin.

E. I cannot dispute that.

A. How stands it then? Is that itself to be deemed a light
punishment: that lust should be master, and draw this way
and that a mind beggared and helpless, despoiled of its wealth
of virtue; now accepting false things for true, now and again
even defending them; now rejecting what it accepted before,
but none the less rushing into new error; now fearful of all
clear reasoning and withholding its assent; now despairing of
all discovery of truth and cowering deep within the lurking
places of folly; now struggling toward the light of understanding, and anon falling back in weariness: and all the
while there rages that tyrannic reign of lusts, and the whole
soul of the man is tossed by changing and conflicting storms:
hither by fear, thither by longing; hither by anxiety, thither
by empty and feigned delight; hither by torment of losing
something dear, thither by eagerness to get what it has not;
hither by the pains of injury received, thither by the fires of

vengeance. Turn where you will: avarice heaps up and extravagance wastes; ambition lures and pride puffs up; he is tortured by envy and buried in sloth, goaded by obstinacy and harassed by inferiority; and so with all the other countless things that throng and busy themselves in that kingdom of the lusts. Can we then reckon that no punishment, which, as you see, all must suffer who do not cling to wisdom?

23. *E.* Great indeed do I think that punishment, and altogether just for one who, placed on the heights of wisdom, elects to descend thence and to become the slave of lust. But it is not certain whether there could be such a one, who could will or who does will to do so. For while we believe that man was so perfectly constituted by God, and placed in a state so happy, that only by his own will did he fall to the hardships of this mortal life, yet while I hold this with steadfast faith, I have not reached an understanding of it. I am nowise inclined to grant that your opening up the discussion, if you can, should be postponed.

CHAPTER XII

They who serve lust deservedly suffer the punishments of mortal life, even if they have never been wise.

For what indeed disturbs me greatly is why we should suffer bitter punishments like that—we, who though surely unwise, have never been wise; so that we cannot be said to suffer them deservedly for having forsaken the stronghold of virtue and chosen slavery to lust. So that if you are able to clear that up by discussion, I will on no account agree to postpone it. *A.* You say that as though you considered it clearly proved that we never were wise; you are thinking of the time since we were born into this life. But wisdom belongs to the soul; and whether before its union with this body the soul may have lived another kind of life somewhere else, and lived wisely, is a great and obscure question that must be considered in its proper place. Nevertheless, what we have to

hand is not hindered from being cleared up as far as we can.
25. I ask you, then, have we a will of any sort?

E. I do not know.

A. Do you want to know?

E. I do not know that either.

A. Then do not question me further.

E. Why?

A. Because I ought not to answer your questions unless you have the will to know what you ask. Then again, unless you have the will to attain wisdom, there is no use talking to you about things of this sort. Finally, you cannot be my friend unless you would that it be well with me. Again, surely, as to yourself, see whether you have no will for a happy life of your own.

E. I confess: it cannot be denied that we have a will. Go on now, and let us see what you will make of it.

A. I will do so. But tell me first whether you think you have a good will.

E. What is a good will?

A. A will by which we seek to live uprightly and honorably, and to attain supreme wisdom. See only whether you do not seek an upright and honorable life. Either you do not seek earnestly to be wise, or you will not venture to deny that when we wish these things we have a good will.

E. I deny nothing; and so admit that I have not only a will, but also a good will.

A. What value, pray, do you set on this will? Do you think that wealth, or honors, or bodily delights, or all of these together, are in any way to be placed beside it?

E. God forefend such impious madness!

A. Ought we not to be a little glad that we have that in the soul—I mean this same good will—in comparison with which the things I have named are as naught: things for whose acquiring we see a multitude of men shrink from no labors, no perils?

E. Glad indeed, and greatly.

A. How then of those that taste not this joy? Think you their loss of so great a good is a slight thing?

E. Nay indeed, the very greatest.

26. *A.* So you see now, I think, that it lies in our own will whether we enjoy or miss a good so great and so real. For what more truly lies within the will than the will itself? So that he who has a good will has surely that which far outweighs all kingdoms and all earthly things or bodily delights. But he who has it not lacks forthwith that one thing, which far excelling all good things that lie beyond our controlling, the will alone through itself can give. And so while he deems himself most wretched who has lost a glorious reputation, or vast riches, or all manner of bodily goods; will you not judge that other man most wretched, who though all such things abound to him, as may slip away while he clings to them, and which he may not possess as he will, yet lacks that good will with which these things are not to be compared, and which, though it be a good so great, needs only to be willed to be possessed?

E. Truly.

A. Rightly and deservedly therefore are foolish men, even if they never were wise (for that is undertain, and very obscure) visited by unhappiness like that.

E. I agree.

CHAPTER XIII

By the will we live a happy life: by the will an unhappy one.

27. *A.* Consider now whether you would say that prudence is a knowledge of what to seek and what to avoid.

E. I think so.

A. And is not fortitude that habit of the soul that makes us despise all misfortune or loss of things not subject to our control?

E. So I should say.

A. Moreover temperance is that habit that curbs and restrains the base cravings of our appetites. Or do you think differently?

E. Nay, I am of your opinion.

A. Then there is justice. What else can we call it but the virtue by which each is given his own?

E. I have no other notion of justice.

A. Therefore let him who has a good will, the praises of which we have been singing at such length, embrace this one virtue with an affection that counts naught better. In this let him find his delight; in this, in short, let him rejoice and be glad. When we consider justice and its grandeur, and how it cannot against his will be taken from him by force or craft, can we doubt that such a man is set against all things that are foes to this one good?

E. He must be set against them utterly.

A. Shall we not think him endowed with prudence, who sees to seek this good, and to shun the things at war with it?

E. I do not see how anyone can do that who has not prudence.

A. Right: but why not allow him fortitude also? For surely he cannot love those things that lie beyond our control. For such things are loved by an evil will, which he must resist as if it were the enemy of his dearest good. But loving them not, he laments not their loss, and altogether despises them. For this, as has been said and conceded, he must have fortitude.

E. Let us allow it surely; for I know not who could be more truly called strong than he who with an equal and tranquil mind forgoes those things which it is in us neither to acquire nor hold; and we have shown beyond doubt that he does this.

A. See now whether we can deprive him of temperance, since this is the virtue that is the curb of lust. For what is so hostile to a good will as lust? From which you see clearly that this lover of his own good will resists and opposes his lusts in every way, and is therefore with right called temperate.

E. I agree, proceed.

A. There remains justice. How it can be lacking to him I do not well see. For he who rejoices in the possession of a good will, and opposes, as we have said, those things which are at war with it, cannot wish evil to anyone. It follows therefore that he does hurt to no one; which cannot be except he give to each his own. But when I said that these things are in the nature of justice, I think you will remember that you agreed.

E. I remember indeed, and I acknowledge that in this man who loves and prizes his own good will we shall find all those four virtues you have just described, I agreeing thereto.

28. A. Is there any reason then why we should not admit that the life of such a man is deserving of praise?

E. Absolutely none: rather indeed do all things urge and force us to admit it.

A. How about an unhappy life? Can you possibly imagine that we should not flee from it?

E. Nay, I feel most strongly that we should, and do not think there is anything else to do.

A. But you think indeed that we should not flee from a praiseworthy life.

E. On the contrary, I think we should seek it zealously.

A. The life that is praiseworthy is not then unhappy.

E. That is very clear.

[A. There is now, so far as I think no difficulty left for you to agree that that life, surely, which is not unhappy, is happy?

E. That is most clear.]

A. It is agreed then that the happy man is the lover of his own good will, who in comparison with it despises all those so-called goods, whose loss could befall even if the will to keep them were there.

E. Why not be agreed; since it follows necessarily from what has already been granted?

A. You understand well. But tell me, pray, is not the very loving of a good will, and prizing it as highly as we have described, itself too a good will?

E. You speak truly.

A. But if we rightly judge this man to be happy, do we not rightly judge him unhappy who is of a contrary will?

E. Most rightly.

A. What reason then is there for doubting that, even if we have never been wise before, it is by will that we earn and live a good and happy life; by will a base and wretched one?

E. I admit that we have reached this conclusion by sure and indisputable arguments.

29. *A.* Here is another argument. You recall, I believe, what we said of a good will: we said, I think, that it was one by which we seek to live honorably and uprightly.

E. I remember.

A. If then we love and embrace this will likewise with a good will, and prize it above all those things that we cannot keep simply by wanting to, our reasoning has shown that those virtues will necessarily dwell in the soul, which to possess is itself to live uprightly and honorably. Thus we see that whosoever wills to live uprightly and honorably, if his will for this is greater than his desire for fleeting goods, attains so easily to so great a thing that to possess his will is naught other than himself to will it.

E. I say to you truly, I can hardly keep from shouting for joy, at seeing rise before me a good so great, and founded on a thing so simple.

A. But now this very joy which springs from the attainment of this good, since it lifts up the soul in peace and quiet and steadfastness, is said to be the blessed life; unless you think that living happily is something other than the rejoicing in goods true and sure.

E. I feel as you do.

CHAPTER XIV

Why do so few become happy, when all desire to?

30. *A.* Rightly: but do you not think that every man elects and desires a happy life?

E. Who doubts that every man so wishes?

A. Why then do not all achieve it? For we have said and agreed that it is by wishing it that men deserve it; by wishing also they deserve a wretched one; and so what they get, they deserve. But now appears some sort of conflict, and unless we consider carefully it will arise to trouble our earlier reasoning, solid and careful as that was. For how does anyone suffer an unhappy life, when no one at all wishes to live in misery? Or how can it be that man attains a happy life by wanting it, when all men want to be happy and so many are unhappy? Is it not because it is one thing to want good things or bad, and another to earn a thing by a good or a bad will? For those who are happy, who also ought to be good, are not happy because they wish to be happy, for the wicked wish that too; but because they wish to live rightly, which the wicked do not want to do. Wherefore it is no wonder that the wicked do not achieve what they want; that is, a happy life. For they do not likewise want that which goes with a happy life, and without which no one is worthy of it or attains it. For by that eternal law, to the consideration of which it is now time to return, it is established in immutable stability that desert is in the will, but in happiness and misery are reward and punishment. And so when we say that men are unhappy by reason of their will, we do not on that account say that they want to be unhappy; but that they are in that state of will where unhappiness must follow even if they are unwilling. Wherefore it does not conflict with our earlier reasoning that all wish to be happy, but cannot; for not all wish to live rightly, to which wish alone a happy life is due. But perhaps you have some objection?

E. Not I, indeed.

CHAPTER XV

The eternal law and the temporal; to whom and to what extent they apply.

31. But now let us see how these things are related to that question about the two laws.

A. Very well: but tell me first whether he who loves to live uprightly, and so rejoices in it that it is not only right for him, but sweet and cheerful, loves and holds dear this law by which he sees a happy life given to a good will, and an unhappy life to a bad one?

E. He loves it earnestly and utterly; for it is by follwing that very law that he lives.

A. Well, when he loves that law, does he love something changing and temporal, or fixed and eternal?

E. Eternal, surely, and changeless.

A. How about those who, persisting in an evil will, desire none the less to be happy? Can they love that law by which unhappiness is deservedly meted out to such men?

E. Not at all, I think.

A. Do they then love nothing else?

E. Nay, many things indeed: that is, those things in the getting and holding of which the evil will persists.

A. I suppose you mean riches, honors, sensuous delights, bodily beauty, and all those other things that men desiring may yet fail to win, or may lose when they fain would hold them?

E. Those very things.

A. Seeing these things exposed to the vicissitudes of time, would you deem them eternal?

E. Who would think that, were he ever so mad?

A. Since therefore it is evident that some men love the eternal things and others the temporal, and since it is agreed that there are two laws, the one eternal, the other temporal: knowing anything of equity, which class of men would you place under the eternal law, and which under the temporal?

E. I think what you ask is obvious; for those happy ones, because of their love of things eternal, act under the eternal law; but to the unhappy I think the temporal law applies. *A.* You judge rightly—so long as you firmly believe what reason has now most clearly shown: that they who serve the temporal law cannot be free from that eternal law, from which are derived, as we have said, all things just, or justly changed. You know well, it seems, that they who of their own good will abide by the eternal law have no need of the temporal.

E. I understand.

32. *A.* The eternal law, therefore, commands us to turn away our love from temporal things, and to turn it, purified, to things eternal.

E. It does indeed.

A. What then do you think the temporal law commands, if not that those things that may be called ours at a time when men through cupidity cling to them, may be possessed according to those rights which maintain peace and human fellowship, so far as in such things is possible. These things are moreover: first, this body and what are called its goods; as sound health, keen senses, strength, beauty, and other things, some of which are needed in the useful arts, and on that account more highly valued, others of less worth. Next, freedom: this indeed is no true freedom except for the blessed who abide by the eternal law; but I am speaking here of that freedom in which they think themselves free who have no master, and which they desire who would be released from human masters. Then parents, brothers, wife, children, kindred, relatives, friends, and whoever may be tied to us by some bond of intimacy. Then the state itself, which we are wont to consider a sort of parent; honors too, and reputation, and what is known as popular favor. Finally, property; under which term are comprised all those things of which we are the rightful owners, and which we have the power to give away or sell. To explain how that law distributes to each his

own would be difficult and tedious, and clearly not relevant
to our purpose. It is enough to see that the power exercised
by this law extends only to the taking away of some or all
of these things from those whom it punishes. Thus it keeps
order by fear, and to gain its end racks and tortures the spirits
of those unhappy ones whom it is adapted to rule. For while
they fear to lose these things they observe in their use a
certain moderation, suited to the bonds of a society such as
can be constituted by men of this sort. For they are not
punished for the sin of loving these things, but only for dis-
honestly taking them away from others.

See now whether we have not reached that goal which you
thought so distant. For we started to inquire how far that law
which govern states and peoples has a right to punish.

E. I see that we have reached it.

33. *A.* You see also that no punishment could be inflicted on
men, either by wrong done them, or by vengeance taken on
them for some wrong, if they did not love those things which
can be taken from them against their will.

E. I see that too.

A. You see, therefore, that the same things may be put to a
bad use by one, and to a good use by another. And he who
uses them for ill clings with love to them and is entangled by
them; that is to say he is subject to what should be subject to
him, and makes those things his goods for whose right ordering and good use he himself must needs be good. But he
who uses these things rightly shows that they are indeed
goods, but not for him; for they do not make him better, but
rather are by him made good. And so let him not cleave to
them with love, or make them members of his soul, which
loving them would do; lest when they begin to be cut off he
be deformed by pain and wasting. But let him be lifted far
above them; ready to possess and rule such things when needs
be, and readier yet to lose and not possess. Since then these
things are so, think you to indict silver and gold because of
avaricious men, or food because of gluttons, or wine because

of drunkards, or women's forms because of fornicators and adulterers? And so with all other things: just as you may see both the physician using fire to heal, and the poisoner using bread for crime.

E. It is true indeed. Not things themselves are to be blamed, but the men who use them for ill.

CHAPTER XVI

Concluding remarks on the question considered.

34. *A.* Very well. We have begun to see, I think, how strong is eternal law, and have found to what extent the temporal law can go in punishing; and have distinguished pretty clearly the two kinds of things, the eternal and the temporal, and also the two kinds of men, the one loving and following the eternal things, and the other the temporal; and have seen that what each man chooses to follow and embrace is fixed in the will, and that only by the will can the mind be deposed from its lawful station and its stronghold taken. And it is clear that things themselves are not to blame when someone makes bad use of them, but only he who so uses them. So now let us return, if you will, to the question raised at the beginning of this discussion, and see whether it is solved. For we began by asking what it is to do evil, and from this question has come all that we have said. Wherefore we may now turn our attention to it, and consider whether to do evil is aught else than to neglect eternal things, which are perceived and enjoyed by the mind itself, and which while it loves them it cannot lose; and to follow as if they were great and wonderful those temporal things that are perceived through the senses of man's meaner part, the body. For in this one kind I think all evil deeds, that is all sins, are included. But I would like to hear what you think.

35. *E.* It is as you say, and I agree: all sins are contained in this one kind; when one is turned away from things divine and truly enduring, and turned to things changing and unsure.

For though these latter are rightly placed in their own order, and display a certain beauty of their own, it is none the less a mark of a perverted and disordered mind to be a slave to their pursuit; for the mind is by divine right and ordinance set above them to bend them to its will. And I see that we have at the same time solved that other problem—why we do wrong—which we undertook in consequence of the first—what wrong-doing is. For if I mistake not our orderly reasoning has shown that we do it by the free choice of our will. But I would ask whether that free choice itself, by which we are shown to have the power to sin, should have been given to us by Him who made us. For lacking it we would seem not to be liable to sin; and it is to be feared that God may thus be judged to be the author also of our evil deeds.

A. Have no fear whatever of that. But we must take another time to examine that more thoroughly. For this discussion must needs be rounded off; I would have you believe that by it we have, as it were, knocked at the door to the study of great and obscure matters. When, God leading us, we shall begin to reach their profundities, you will indeed see what a difference there is between this disputation and those which are to follow; how much those will surpass it, not only in the acuteness of their inquiry, but also in their sublimity of matter, and in the dazzling light of their truth. May only piety enough be ours, so that divine Providence will permit us to hold and finish the course we have begun.

E. I yield to your will; and with all my heart second it with my own wish and judgment.

BOOK TWO

WHEREIN, A DIFFICULTY HAVING ARISEN FROM THE FACT THAT
THE FREEDOM OF THE WILL WHEREWITH WE SIN IS GIVEN BY
GOD, THESE THREE QUESTIONS ARE STUDIED: FIRST, BY WHAT
REASONING IS IT CLEAR THAT GOD EXISTS; SECOND, WHETHER
ALL GOODS ARE FROM GOD; THIRD, WHETHER FREE WILL IS TO
BE ACCOUNTED A GOOD.

CHAPTER I

Why freedom, by which men sin, is given by God.

1. E. Explain to me now, if it can be done, why God gave man
free judgment of will, when certainly, if he had not received
it, he would not be able to sin.

A. You are perfectly sure, then, that God gave man this
thing, which you think should not have been given?

E. So far as I think I understood the earlier discussion, we
both have free will, and could not sin without it.

A. I too remember now that that was made clear. But now I
am asking whether you know that God gave this thing which
we know we have, and without which we could not sin.

E. No one else, I think. For from Him we are; and sinning
or doing right, from Him we earn our punishment or reward.

A. I would like to know whether you know this clearly, or
whether prompted by authority you are ready to believe it,
even if you do not know it.

E. I confess that I first trusted authority in the matter. But
what is more true than that all good things are from God,
and hat all just things are good, and that it is just to punish
sinners and to reward well-doers? From which it follows that
from God sinners are visited by unhappiness, and righteous
men by happiness.

2. A. I am not objecting, but I am asking that other question:
How do you know that we are from Him? For you did not

explain that just now, but only why we merit from Him punishment or reward.

E. That too I think is clear, if for no other reason than that it has been shown that God punishes sins; since, indeed, all justice is from Him. For though it is of the nature of some goodness not to bestow its benefits upon aliens, yet is it not of the nature of justice to take vengeance upon aliens. Whence it is clear that we belong to Him, who is not only most generous in giving, but also most just in punishing. Then too, from what I averred and you conceded, that every good is from God, it may be argued that man too is from God. For man himself, in so far as he is man, is something good, because he can live rightly if he will.

A. Clearly, if these things are so, the question you proposed is answered. For if man is something good, and cannot be unless he wills to live rightly, he ought to have a free will; for without it he would not be able to do right. For though we sin also by that will, it is not to be believed that God gave free will for that purpose. It is a sufficient reason why it should have been given, that without it man could not live rightly. But that it was given for this purpose may be seen from this: that if anyone shall have used it for sinning, he incurs divine punishment. And this would be unjust, if free will had been given not only for right living, but also for sinning. For how could he be justly punished who should use his will for that for which it was given.

But now when God punishes the sinner, does He not say, in effect: "Why have you not used your free will for that for which I gave it to you; that is, for doing right?" Then again, if man were without freedom of the will, what would become of that good for which justice itself is commended, in condemning sins and rewarding well-doing? And thus both punishment and reward would be unjust, if man had not a free will; for that would be neither a sin nor a good deed which were not done willingly. But there should be justice both in punishment and reward, since justice is one of the goods that are from God. Therefore God should have given man a free will.

CHAPTER II

Objection: if free will was given for good, why can it be bent toward evil?

4. E. I grant now that God gave it. But does it not seem to you, I ask, that if it has been given for doing right, we should not be able to pervert it to a sinful use? Like justice, which too is given to man for right living—for could anyone live evilly by his own justice? So no one would be able to sin by his will, if that will had been given him to do right.

A. God will grant, I hope, that I shall be able to answer you; or rather that you yourself will find the answer from that greatest teacher of all, the truth within your own heart. But I would have you tell me briefly if you have sure knowledge of what I asked you, that God gave us free will; whether or not we conclude that God should not have given that which we acknowledge that He gave. For if it is not certain that He did give it, we may rightly ask whether it was well given, so that when we find that it was well given, we will also find that it was given by Him who gave all goods to men: if on the other hand we find it not well given, we shall know that it was not given by Him whom to blame were impious. But if it is certain that He himself gave it, however it was given we must acknowledge that it neither should not have been given, nor given otherwise than as it was given. For He gave it whose act can nowise be rightly censured.

5. E. Though I hold these things with unshaken faith, yet since I do not hold them by knowledge, let us inquire into them as if all were uncertain. For I see that as it is uncertain whether free will was given us for doing right, since we can also sin by it, that other question becomes also uncertain, whether it should have been given. But if it is uncertain that it was given for doing right, and also uncertain whether it should have

been given, it is not certain that it was given by Him whom it were impious to believe had given anything He should not have given.

A. At least you are certain that God exists?

E. Even that I do not hold by reason, but by steadfast faith.

A. If then one of those fools of whom it is written: *The fool hath said in his heart, There is no God,** should say this to you, and not be willing to believe what you believe, but want to know whether you were believing the truth; would you leave the man, or would you think that in some way he should be persuaded of what you so firmly believe; especially if he had the will not to oppose it obstinately, but wished eagerly to know?

E. What you said last advises me well enough as to how I should answer him. For however unreasonable he might be, he would admit that nothing whatever, and least of all so great a matter, should be urged about insincerely or with obstinacy. This granted, he would first try to concince me that he was asking in good faith, and that he had no hidden guile or obstinacy about the matter.

Then I should show (as I think anyone could easily do) that since he himself was demanding that matters hidden in his own mind be believed by another who did not know them, that it would be only reasonable for him to believe that God exists, from the books of those great men who have left written testimony that they lived with the Son of God, and who have written also of things seen by them which could not possibly be if there were no God: and he would be a simple fellow indeed to criticize me for believing those men when he wanted me to believe him. But that which he could not rightly object to he could in no wise make an excuse for his unwillingness to imitate.

A. If then, as to whether God exists, it is enough for you that it should not seem unreasonable to believe those great

---

*Psalm XIII, 1.

men, why, pray, do you not think we should likewise take on
the authority of those same men all those other things which
we subjected to inquiry as if they were unsure and not clearly
known? We should then have to trouble no further to examine them.

E. But that which we believe, we desire also to know and
understand.

6. A. You remember rightly; we cannot go back on the position
we took at the beginning of our former discussion. For believing is one thing, and understanding another; and we must
first believe whatever great and divine matter we desire to
understand. Else would the Prophet have said in error, *Except
ye believe, ye shall not understand.** Then too our Lord himself, both by His words and His acts, exhorted those whom
He called to salvation to first believe. But afterwards, when
He spoke of the gift itself that was to be given to believers,
He did not say, "This moreover is eternal life, that ye believe," but, *This is life eternal, that they might know thee the
only true God, and Jesus Christ, whom thou hast sent.*†
Again, He says to believers, *Seek and ye shall find.*‡ But one
cannot speak of that being found which is believed without
knowledge, nor does anyone become prepared to find God
who does not first believe that which he is afterward to know.
Wherefore, following our Lord's precepts, let us seek earnestly. For what He himself encourages us to seek, that same
shall we find by His showing, so far as such things may be
found in this life, and by such as we. For it is to be believed
that these things are seen more clearly and known more
perfectly by those better than we, even while they live on
earth, and certainly by the good and pious after this life. And
so we must hope it will be with us, and despising things
earthly and mortal must love and desire these things in
every way.

---

*Isaiah VII, 9; In the Vulgate, *permanebitis* for *intelligetis*.
†John, XVII, 3.
‡Matt. VII, 7.

CHAPTER III

That it may become evident that God exists, it is inquired what is most excellent in man.

7.   Let us then pursue the following order of inquiry: first, how is it manifest that God is; next, whether goods, whatsoever their kind or degree, are from Him; finally, whether free will is to be accounted a good. When we have answered these it will be clear enough, I think, whether free will was rightly given to man. Wherefore, in order that we may take our start from the most obvious things, I ask you whether you yourself exist, or whether you think you may be under an illusion as to that; although surely if you did not exist you could not possibly have an illusion.

E. Go on rather to other matters.

A. It is evident, then, that you exist; and since that could not be evident unless you were living, it is also evident that you live. Do you understand that these two things are very true?

E. I understand thoroughly.

A. Therefore this third thing is evident: you understand.

E. It is evident.

A. Which of these three do you think is most excellent?

E. Understanding.

A. Why do you think so?

E. Because while there are three things: to exist, to live, to understand; even a stone exists, and a beast lives, yet I do not think that a stone lives, or that a beast understands. But he who understands assuredly both exists and lives; wherefore I do not hesitate to judge that one more excellent in which all three are present, than that in which two or one are lacking. For though what lives certainly also exists, it does not follow that it also understands: of such sort, I judge, is the life of a beast. If something exists moreover, it by no means follows that it lives and understands; for I may acknowledge that a corpse exists, but no one would say that it lives. But if the thing does not live, much less does it understand.

A. We see then that of these three, two are wanting to the corpse, one to the beast, and none to man.

E. True.

A. We also hold that to be most excellent of the three which man has with the two others; namely, understanding, whose possession implies both existence and life.

E. Surely.

8. *A.* Tell me now, whether you know that you have those everyday bodily senses: seeing and hearing, and smelling, and tasting, and touching?

E. I do.

A. What do you think pertains to the sense of sight; I mean what do you think we perceive by sight?

E. Anything corporeal.

A. Do you think we also perceive hardness and softness by sight?

E. No.

A. What then properly pertains to the eyes, and is perceived by them?

E. Color.

A. What to the ears?

E. Sound.

A. What to smell?

E. Odor.

A. What to taste?

E. Flavor.

A. What to touch?

E. Softness and hardness, smoothness and roughness, and many such things.

A. How about the shapes of bodies: large, small, square, round, and such? Do we not perceive them both by touch and by sight, so that we cannot properly assign them either to touch or sight alone, but only to both?

E. That is clear.

A. You see then that certain senses have individually their own proper objects about which they tell us, and that certain others have some objects in common.

E. I see that too.

A. Now can we by means of any of these senses distinguish what is proper to each sense, and what all or certain senses have in common?

E. By no means: we judge that by a sort of interior sense.

A. Is that perhaps reason itself, which the beasts have not? For it is by reason, I think, that we grasp these things, and so know that we have senses.

E. I think rather that by reason we comprehend that there is a certain interior sense, to which all things are referred by the five ordinary senses. For the sense by which a beast sees is one thing, and that by which it seeks or avoids what it perceives by sight is another; for the first sense is in the eyes, but that other is in the soul itself. By it animals seek and appropriate what they like, and avoid and reject what they do not; not only what they see, but what they hear or perceive by the other senses. Nor can this sense be called sight or hearing or smell or taste or touch, but is something other that presides over all of them together. While we comprehend this by reason, as I have said, we cannot nevertheless call it reason, since the beasts also evidently have it.

9. *A.* I recognize that, whatever it is, and do not hesitate to call it the interior sense. But unless it goes beyond what is brought to us by our bodily senses, it cannot attain to knowledge. For what we know, we hold in the grasp of reason. But, not to mention other things, we know that we cannot perceive colors by hearing, nor voices by sight. And when we know this, we know it neither by our eyes nor by our ears, nor by that interior sense which the beasts also have. For one cannot believe that they know that ears do not perceive light, nor eyes voices, since we discern such things only by rational attention and thought.

E. I cannot say that I see that clearly. For what if they do discern also by that interior sense, which you admit they have, that colors cannot be perceived by hearing, nor voices by sight?

A. Well, do you think that they can distinguish from one another the color that is perceived, and the sense that is in the eye, and that interior sense within the soul, and the reason by which these are defined and enumerated one by one?

E. By no means.

A. Could reason, then, distinguish these four from one another, and set bounds to them by definitions, if color were not referred to it by the sense of the eyes, and that sensation again by the interior sense that presides over it, and that same interior sense by itself, assuming that there is not yet another something interposed?

E. I do not see how else it could.

A. And do you see that color is perceived by the sense of the eyes, but that the sensation itself is not perceived by the same sense? For you do not see the seeing itself by the same sense by which you see color.

E. Not at all.

A. Try also to distinguish these; for I think you will not deny that color is one thing, and seeing color another, and that it is yet another, when color is not present, to have the sense by which it could be seen if it were present.

E. I distinguish those too, and grant that they are different.

A. Do you see any of these three with your eyes, except color?

E. Nothing else.

A. Tell me then how you do see the other two; for if you did not see them, you could not distinguish them.

E. I know nothing further. I know that I do, nothing more.

A. You do not know then whether this is reason itself, or that life which we call the interior sense, and which is superior to the bodily senses, or something else?

E. No.

A. You know at least that these things can be defined only

by reason; and that reason cannot do this unless they are
presented to it for examination.

E. That is true.

A. Whatever, therefore, that other thing is, by means of
which we perceive everything that we know, it is in the service
of reason, to which it presents and reports whatever it touches,
so that the things perceived may be distinguished by their
properties, and grasped not merely for perception, but for
knowledge as well.

E. That is so.

A. Well, how about this reason, which distinguishes from
one another its servants and the things they bring before it,
and likewise recognizes the difference between itself and these
things, and assures itself of its superiority to them? Does it
comprehend itself by means of anything other than itself, that
is, reason? Or would you know that you had reason if you
did not perceive it by reason?

E. Most true.

A. So then, when we perceive a color we do not likewise by
the sense itself perceive that we perceive; nor when we hear
a sound do we also hear our hearing; nor when we smell a
rose has the smelling fragrance too; nor tasting something
does the tasting itself have flavor in the mouth; nor touching
a thing can we also touch the sense of touch. Therefore it is
clear that those five senses cannot be perceived by any one
sense among them, although by them all corporeal things are
perceived.

E. That is clear.

CHAPTER IV

*The interior sense perceives that it perceives; whether it also
distinguishes itself or not.*

10. *A.* I think it is clear that the interior sense perceives not only
the things referred to it by the five senses, but also the
sensations themselves. For otherwise an animal would not
stir, either to pursue or to run away from anything, if it did

not perceive that it had the sensation—not as knowledge, for that is reason's province, but only in order to move—which it certainly does not perceive by any one of those five. If this is still not clear, it will become clear by considering some one sense, say sight. For one could not open his eyes, or turn his gaze upon what he seeks to see, unless when his eyes were closed, or not turned toward it, he perceived that he did not see. But if, not seeing, he perceives that he does not see, he must also perceive that he sees when he does see; for the fact that when he sees a thing he does not move his eyes in searrh of it shows that he perceives both.

But whether this life that perceives that it perceives corporeal things perceives itself too, is not so clear; except that anyone who looks within himself finds that every living thing flees death. But since death is the opposite of life, it must be that life perceives itself, since it flees its own opposite. But if this be still not clear, let us pass it over, so that we may move on toward our goal only by evidence that is certain and manifest. For this much is clear: we perceive corporeal things by our bodily senses, but we cannot by the sense itself perceive a sense. By the interior sense we perceive both that we are perceiving corporeal things through the bodily sense, and also the bodily sense itself. But by reason all those other things and also reason itself become known and are held together in knowledge. Is this clear to you?

E. Perfectly clear.

A. Tell me now, how did this problem arise, over which, in our search for a solution, we have tarried so long on this road?

CHAPTER V

The interior sense is superior to the external senses, of which it is a regulator and judge.

11. E. So far as I recall, we are still considering the first of those three questions which we proposed a little while ago in arranging the order of this discussion; namely, how can that

be made evident which we must anyhow believe most firmly and steadfastly—that God exists.

A. You are quite right. But I want you also to keep carefully in mind that when I asked you whether you knew that you yourself existed, not only was that clear to us, but also two other propositions.

E. I remember that too.

A. See now to which of those three you think pertains everything that is touched by our bodily senses; that is, under which head would you put whatever reaches our senses through the eyes, or through any other instrument of the body. Is it in the class which just exists, or in that which also lives, or in that which also understands?

E. In that which just exists.

A. How about the sense itself? In which class of the three do you think it is?

E. In that which lives.

A. Which now of these two do you judge to be the better: the sense itself, or what the sense perceives?

E. The sense, of course.

A. Why?

E. Because that which lives is better than that which merely is.

12. *A.* How about the interior sense? It is below reason, to be sure, and our earlier investigations have shown that we share it with the beasts. But would you hesitate to rank it above the senses by which we perceive bodies, and which you have just said are to be ranked above the bodies themselves?

E. I should not hesitate at all.

A. I should like also to hear from you why you do not hesitate. For you will not be able to say now that the interior sense should be put in that one of the three classes which also understands, but it must still go in the class that exists and lives, albeit without understanding; for the beasts, who have no understanding, have this sense. This being the case, I ask why you prefer the interior sense to the sense by which bodies are perceived, since both belong to the class that lives. For you placed the sense by which we perceive bodies above those bodies because they are in the class that merely exists, while it is in the class that also lives; so that when you find the interior sense also in that class, tell me why you think it superior. For if you say it is because the one perceives the other, I do not believe you will be able to find a rule by which we can establish that everything that perceives is better than that which is perceived by it; lest perhaps we should thence be constrained to say that everything that understands is better than that which is understood by it. But this is false: because man understands wisdom, but he is not better than wisdom itself. See therefore, for what reason it appears to you that the interior sense is to be preferred to those senses by which we perceive bodies.

E. Because I perceive the former to be a sort of regulator and judge of the latter. For if anything is lacking in the performance of its office, it is demanded of it as a service owing, as was argued a little while ago. For the sense of the eyes does not see that it sees, or that it does not see; and not seeing this, cannot judge what is lacking, or what is sufficient. But the interior sense tells the soul of the beast when to open closed eyes, and perceives when they are supplied with what was lacking. But there is no doubt that he who judges is superior to him whom he judges.

A. Do you see too that those bodily senses also judge of bodies after a fashion? For pleasure and pain are their affairs, as when they are touched gently or roughly by a body. For just as the interior sense judges what is lacking or sufficient in the sense of the eyes, so the sense itself of the eyes judges what is lacking or sufficient in colors. So too, just as the interior sense judges our hearing, whether or not it be sufficiently alert, our hearing itself judges of voices, when they breathe softly, and when they grate harshly. There is no need to run through the other bodily senses, for now you perceive, I think, what I want to say; namely, that the interior sense

judges those bodily senses, approving their integrity or demanding what they owe; and in like manner the bodily senses
themselves judge of bodies, appropriating their light touch
and rejecting the opposite.

E. I see clearly, and most heartily agree.

CHAPTER VI

Reason is more excellent than all else in man: if there is any-
thing more excellent, it is God.

13. *A.* Consider now whether reason judges the interior sense.
For I do not ask whether you think it is better, because I
have no doubt that you do—though for that matter I do not
think it need be asked whether reason judges this sense. For
in those very things that are below it, that is, in bodies and
the bodily senses and in the interior sense, what indeed but
reason tells us how one thing is better than another, and that
it itself is superior to them; and this it certainly could not do
if it did not judge them.

E. That is evident.

A. Since, therefore, a nature that neither lives nor understands, but only is, such as a dead body, is surpassed by a
nature such as the soul of a beast, which not only is, but lives
too, though it does not understand; and this again is surpassed
by one that is and lives and understands, such as the rational
mind of man; do you think you can discover in us, that is,
among those things that go to make up our nature as men,
anything more excellent than that which we have placed
highest among these three? For it is clear that we have a
body, and a certain vital principle by which that body lives
and grows, which two we recognize also in the beasts; and a
third something which the beast's nature has not—a sort of
head or eye of the soul, not to think of a more appropriate
name for reason and understanding. So pray see whether you
can find anything in man's nature higher than reason.

E. I see nothing at all better.

14. *A.* What if we could find something of which you were sure, not only that it exists, but also that it is more excellent than our reason? Would you hesitate, whatever it might be, to call it God?

E. I do not see why, if I can find something that is better than what is best in my own nature, I should say that it is God. For I do not like to call that God to which my own reason is inferior, but only Him than whom none is higher.

A. Clearly so: for He himself has given to this reason of yours the power to feel thus reverently and truly about Him. But, I would ask, if you find nothing above our reason but what is eternal and changeless, would you hesitate to call that God? For you know that bodies are changeable; and clearly the very life that animates the body is subject to change with changing conditions; and reason itself, now striving to attain the truth and anon not striving, sometimes attaining it and again not attaining it, is clearly shown to be mutable. So, if without the use of any of the body's instruments—not touch, nor taste, nor smell, nor ears, nor eyes, nor any sense inferior to it, but by itself alone—reason discovers something eternal and immutable, and sees itself as lower, it should acknowledge that to be its God.

E. That one will I plainly acknowledge to be God, than Whom nothing is proved to be higher.

A. Well said. It will be enough then if I show that there is something of that sort, so that you will acknowledge it to be God; or if there is something higher, you will grant that that is God. So that whether there be anything higher or not, it will be proved that God exists when I shall have shown you, with His help, what I assured you was higher than reason.

E. Show me then what you promise.

CHAPTER VII

How the same thing may be perceived by many, either entire or not entire, and at the same time by different persons.

15. *A.* I will do so. But I would first ask whether my bodily senses are the same as yours, or whether mine are in fact mine alone, and yours yours alone; for if this were not the case I could not see anything with my eyes which you did not see.

E. I concede fully, that though they are the same in kind we have each of us his own personal senses—sight, hearing, and all the others. For one man can not only see, but hear what another does not, and perceive by any other sense you will what another does not perceive. Whence it is evident that your senses are yours alone, and mine are mine alone.

A. Would you say the same about the interior sense too, or is there a difference?

E. No difference, surely. For certainly my own interior sense perceives my sensations, and yours perceives yours; so that I am frequently asked by someone who sees something whether I too see it, because only I perceive whether I see it or not, not he who asks me.

A. How about reason: has not each one of us his own? For it may happen that I understand something that you do not; and you cannot know whether I understand, but I know.

E. It is evident that we have each of us individually his own rational mind.

16. *A.* But now will you be able to say too that we have each individual suns which we see, or moons, or morning stars, or such like things; even though it be true that each sees them through his own individual sense?

E. I would never say that.

A. Many of us, therefore, can see one thing at the same time, while the senses through which we perceive the one thing that we see together are separate and individual; so that while my sense is one and yours is another, it can nevertheless happen that what we see is not one mine and another yours, but a single thing, appearing to both of us and seen simultaneously by both.

E. That is very evident.

A. Also we may hear simultaneously some one voice; and although my hearing is one and yours another, yet the voice we hear is not one voice for me and another for you, but whatever has sounded is simultaneously present to both of us as a single and undivided thing to be heard.

E. That too is evident.

17. *A.* But now as to the other bodily senses you must note what we are saying: that in what touches this matter they neither act altogether like those two of the eyes and ears, nor altogether unlike them. For you and I can fill our nostrils from the same air, and perceive its condition by its odor, and likewise can both taste of one honeycomb, or any other food or drink, and perceive its condition by its flavor; and though it is one, our sensations are separate, yours for you and mine for me, so that while we both perceive the same odor or flavor, you do not perceive by my sense nor I by yours, nor by any sense that might be common to both of us; but my sense is utterly mine, and yours is yours, although one odor or one flavor is perceived by both. In this respect, therefore, these two senses are found to have something like those other two, seeing and hearing. But in what pertains to the matter in hand they differ in this: that although we both draw in one air through our nostrils, or take one food in tasting, I do not nevertheless breathe that part of the air which you breathe, nor take the same part of the food as you, but I take one part and you another; so that when I breathe of the whole air I draw in a part such as suffices me, and you likewise from the whole draw in another sufficiency for yourself; and though one entire repast is eaten by both of us, nevertheless it cannot be eaten entire by me and also entire by you, in the way that I hear a whole word and you the same whole word at the

same time, or as what I see of any view you too see at the
same time; but of food or drink one part must pass into me
and another into you. But perhaps this is not clear to you!
E. Nay, rather it is most clear and indubitable.

18. *A.* Do you think now that the sense of touch is to be compared to the senses of the eyes and ears, as regards the question before us? For not only can we both perceive one body
by touching it, but you too can touch the same part of the
body that I have touched, so that we can both perceive by our
touch not only the same body, but the same part of that body.
For with touching it is not the case as with something edible
set before us, where you and I cannot both take all when we
both eat of it; but the same undivided thing that I touch you
too can touch, so that we both touch not each a part, but
each the whole.

E. I admit that in this way the sense of touch is very like
those other two. But it seems unlike in this respect; namely,
that both of us can at one and the same time see or hear one
entire thing: we can indeed also touch at the same time one
entire object, but in different parts—the same part, however,
only at different times; for I can put my touch on no part
which you are touching until you remove your hand.

19. *A.* Carefully answered—but since, of all the things that we
perceive, there are some which both, some which each one
individually may perceive, you ought to see this too: our
sensations themselves are indeed perceived only individually,
so that neither I perceive your sensation, nor you mine. As
regards those things which we perceive with our bodily senses,
what we cannot perceive both, but only individually, is only
that which so becomes our own that we can change it and
turn it into ourselves; like food and drink, of which no part
that I digest can you too digest. For even though nurses do
give masticated food to infants, nevertheless, what the tasting
has taken and converted into the flesh of the chewer can in
no manner be recalled and put back into the food of the child.

For when the palate tastes something pleasant it claims for itself a small but irrevocable part, and compels this to become what accords with the nature of the body. For if this were not the case, no taste would be left in the mouth after those masticated foods were spit out and given back.

This is also true of those parts of the air that we draw in through our nostrils; for even though you too can breathe in some of the air that I have returned, you cannot nevertheless breathe in also that which has gone to nourish me, because that cannot be returned. For physicians teach that we take nourishment through the nostrils also, which nourishment I alone can perceive as I inhale, and cannot restore when I exhale for you too to perceive by breathing it in through your nostrils.

Other sensible things we may perceive as we will, without thereby destroying them and changing them into our bodies. There we may both perceive, either at the same time, or by turns at different times so that either the whole or the part that I perceive is perceived by you also; such are light, or sound, or bodies that we touch without injuring them.

E. I understand.

A. It is clear then, that those things which we do not change and yet perceive by our bodily senses do not belong to the nature of our senses, and hence are more our common possession, because they are not changed into something that is ours exclusively.

E. I thoroughly agree.

A. Therefore that is to be regarded as our own and as it were private possession which is of each one of us alone, and which he alone perceives within himself because it pertains properly to his own nature. That, however, is common, and so to speak public, which is perceived by all percipients without any change or destruction.

E. Just so.

CHAPTER VIII

The reason of numbers is perceived by no bodily sense; by any-one who understands it it is perceived as one and immutable.

20. *A.* Consider now and tell me whether you can find anything which all men, each reasoning with his own mind and reason, may see in common; while that which they see is present to all, and is not converted to the use of those to whom it is present, as are food and drink, but remains whole and un-corrupted, whether they see it or do not see it. Or would you perhaps think that there is nothing of this sort?

E. On the contrary, I think there are many, of which it is enough to mention one. For the reason and truth of numbers waits upon all who reason, so that every calculator may see it, each with his own reason, and endeavor to grasp it with his understanding. And one will do so easily, another with more difficulty, and yet another will be quite unable; although not-withstanding it offers itself to all who have the power to grasp it; nor is it changed and transmuted when anyone per-ceives it into nutriment as it were for the perceiver, nor when one makes a mistake in it is it thereby less, but while it remains true and whole, he is the more in error the less he perceives it.

21. *A.* Quite right: but I see that you answered readily as if not unversed in these things. Nevertheless, if some one should say that these numbers are as it were certain images of visible things, impressed on our mind not by any nature of their own, but by those things that are reached by the senses of the body, —what would you answer? Or do you too think that?

E. I should by no means think that. For even if I have per-ceived numbers by a bodily sense, I cannot thereby perceive by a bodily sense the ratios of partition and combination of numbers. For by this light of the mind I refute him who gives a false result in calculation, either by addition or sub-traction. And I do not know for how long will endure anything that I touch with my bodily senses, such as this sky and this earth, and whatever other bodies I perceive in them. But seven and three are ten, not only now, but always; nor was there ever a time when seven and three were not ten, nor will ever be a time when seven and three will not be ten. I say, therefore, that this incorruptible truth of number is common to me and to any reasoning person whatsoever.

22. *A.* I do not oppose you when you answer so truly and indisputably. But you may also easily see that numbers are not derived from our bodily senses, if you will consider, as to any number, that as many times as it contains one, so many is it called. For example, if it contains one twice it is called two; if thrice, three, and if it contains one ten times it is called ten; and the number of times any number whatever contains one gives it its name, and it is called so much. But anyone who considers the matter aright will certainly find that we cannot perceive one by our bodily senses. For whatever reaches us through such a sense is clearly seen to be not one, but many; for it is body, and therefore has innumerable parts. For—not to trace out finer and even finer divisions—however tiny a particle that body may be, it has certainly a right part and a left part, a top and a bottom, a front and a back, or an outside and an inside; for we might acknowledge that these are present in any body, however tiny its dimensions, and hence we must concede that no body is truly and simply one; although we nevertheless could not enumerate such a many without a separate and distinct knowledge of one. For when I look for one in a body, and when I have no doubt that I do not find it, I know assuredly what I seek there, and what I do not find there, and what cannot be found there, or rather what is not there at all. But whenever I know one I certainly do not know this through my bodily senses, because by the bodily senses we know only body, which we have proved to be not one, pure and simple.

Moreover, if we do not perceive one by a sense of the body, we do not perceive any number by that sense, so far at least as concerns those numbers that we discern by our understanding. For there is no one of them that does not get its name from the number of times it contains one; and one is not perceived by the bodily sense. For the half of any particle makes up a whole of two such halves, and has also its half: therefore those two parts are in the body in such a way that they are not simply two. But on the other hand the *number* that we call two because it contains twice that which is simply one, its half part, is something which is itself simply one, and cannot have a half, or a third, or any part whatsoever, because it is simply and truly one.

23. Then again, whereas taking the numbers in order, after one we get two, which comparing with one we find to be its double; the double of two does not follow in immediate succession, but four, which is the double of two, follows after the interposition of three. And this rule extends to all the other numbers by a most certain and immutable law: that after one, that is after the first of all the numbers, itself excepted, the first is that which contains it twice; for two follows one. But after the second number, that is after two, it is the second, itself excepted, that is the double of it; for the first after two is three, and the second four, the double of the second number. After the third, that is after three, it is the third, itself excepted, that is the double of it; for after the third, that is to say three, the first is four, the second five, and the third six, which is the double of three. So again after the fourth it is the fourth, itself excepted, that is its double; for after the fourth, that is four, the first is five, the second six, the third seven, and the fourth eight, which is the double of four. And so throughout all the other numbers you will find this that has been found in the first pair of numbers, that is, in one and two: that the double of any number is just as many numbers after it as that number itself is from the very beginning.

But now when we perceive this thing to be for all numbers fixed and inviolate, whence comes this perception? For no one has touched all numbers by any sense of the body, for they are innumerable. Whence then do we know this for all, or by what so sure an appearance or image do we know so confidently this truth of number throughout things innumerable, if we do not perceive it by that inner light which the sense of the body knows not?

24.   By this and many like proofs, those to whom God has given an inquiring mind, and who are not blinded by obstinacy, are compelled to acknowledge that the reason and truth of numbers is not related to the bodily sense, and that it is established pure and unalterable for all reasoning men to see in common. Wherefore, while many other things might be thought of which are present and as it were public to reasoning men, and which remain inviolate and changeless while they are perceived by the mind and reason of each individual perceiver; I was yet by no means sorry that the reason and truth of numbers was what first came to your mind when you wished to answer my question. For not for nothing is number joined to wisdom in the Sacred Books, where it is said: *I and my heart have gone round, that I might know, and consider, and inquire the wisdom and the number.**

CHAPTER IX

What wisdom is, without which no one is happy; whether it is one in all wise men.

25.   But I would like to know how you think wisdom itself is to be regarded. Do you think that individual men have each their individual wisdoms, or that one wisdom is present to all in common, and that each is wise in the measure that he partakes of it?

E. I do not know what you call wisdom; for I see, forsooth, that what is said or done wisely seems different to different

---

*Ecclesiastes, VII, 25. The Vulgate has *sapientiam et rationem* instead of *sapientiam et numerum*. There are variant readings of the quotation in different editions. The version here followed is that favored by Migne. (P.L. vol. 32, col. 1254.)

men. For those who go to war seem to themselves to be acting wisely; and those who, disdaining war, devote their care and labor to the cultivation of land, praise this more highly and attribute it to wisdom; and those who are shrewd in devising ways to make money think themselves wise; and those who disregard or put from them all these and such-like temporal things, and devote all their zeal to the investigation of truth, that they may know themselves and God, judge this to be the great reward of wisdom; and those who are loath to give themselves to this leisure of seeking and contemplating truth, but prefer to busy themselves with exacting cares and duties, that they may take counsel with men and be employed in the control and just government of human affairs, think themselves wise; and those who do both of these things, and live partly in the contemplation of truth and partly in official labors, which they think they owe to human society, seem to themselves to hold the palm of wisdom. I omit innumerable sects, of which there is none that, placing its own adherents above all others, does not hold that they alone are wise. Wherefore, since the question before us demands an answer, not as to what we believe, but as to what we hold with clear understanding, I shall be quite unable to reply to your question until I know also by contemplating and discerning reason that which by believing I hold wisdom to be.

A. Do you think that there is any wisdom other than the truth in which the supreme good is discerned and held: For all those sectarians that you have mentioned seek the good; but they are split into different sects because different things seem good to different men. Whoever therefore seeks what he should not seek, even though he seeks what to him seems good, errs notwithstanding. But he who seeks nothing cannot err, nor can he who seeks that which he should seek. In so far therefore as all men seek a happy life, they do not err. But in so far as anyone does not hold to that way of life which leads to happiness, though he acknowledges and professes that he wants only to attain happiness, he errs. For it is error when we follow something which does not lead to that to which we wish to attain. And the more anyone strays in the path of life, the less wise is he; for he is that much farther from that truth in which the supreme good is discerned and known. But if anyone has pursued and attained the supreme good, he is happy; which indisputably we all desire. Therefore, as it is certain that we wish to be happy, so also is it certain that we wish to be wise, because no one is happy without wisdom. But no one is happy except by the supreme good, which is discerned and known in that truth which we call wisdom. And so, just as before we are happy the notion of happiness is yet impressed on our minds, so also before we are wise we have impressed on our minds a notion of wisdom; so that each of us, if he were asked whether he wished to be wise, would reply without a shade of hesitation that he so wished.

27.   Wherefore, since we are now agreed as to what wisdom is, albeit you were not able to explain it in words, (for if you were quite unable to see this with your mind, you could never know both that you wish to be wise, and that you ought so to wish). I would have you tell me whether you think that like the reason and truth of numbers wisdom offers itself to all reasoning men in common; or whether, since there are as many minds as there are men, so that I perceive nothing of your mind, nor you of mine, you think there are also as many wisdoms as there are wise men.

E. If the supreme good is one for all, the truth also in which It is discerned and known, that is wisdom, should be one and common for all.

A.   But do you doubt that the supreme good, whatever it be, is for all men one?

E.   I doubt it indeed; because I see different men taking delight in different things as if they were their supreme goods.

A. I should have wished indeed that no one were in doubt as to the supreme good, just as no one doubts that whatever it is a man cannot be happy until he has attained it. But since this is a large question, and requires perhaps a long discourse, let us assume that there are just as many supreme goods as there are different things themselves, which by different men are sought as their supreme goods; does it then follow that wisdom itself is not one to all in common, because those goods which men discern and choose in it are many and diverse? For if you think this, you may also doubt that the light of the sun is one, because the things we discern by it are many and diverse: from which things each one selects at will that which he would enjoy through his sense of sight; and one man is pleased to look upon the height of some mountain, and rejoices in that sight, another the level surface of a field, another the slopes of the valleys, another the greenness of the woods, another the inconstant evenness of the sea, and another brings together in one view all of these things, or certain of them that are fair, for the joy of regarding them. Just as, therefore, those things are many and diverse which in the light of the sun men behold and choose for their enjoyment, although that light itself is one in which the gaze of each beholder sees and dwells upon that which rejoices it; even so are the goods many and diverse from which each one chooses what he will, and seeing it and holding it for his enjoyment rightly and truly makes it his supreme good; but it may yet be that the light itself of disdom, in which these things are seen and held, is one and common to all wise men.

E. I admit that it may be, and that there is nothing to prevent there being one wisdom common to all, even though the supreme goods be many and various; but I would like to know whether it is so. For what we concede may be so, is not thereby conceded to be so.

A. In the meanwhile we know that there is wisdom; but whether it be one and common to all, or whether individual wise men have their separate wisdoms, as they have their own souls and minds, we do not yet know.

E. That is so.

CHAPTER X

The light of wisdom is one to all wise men in common.

28. *A.* Where then do we see this that we know, whether it be that there is wisdom, or that there are wise men, or that all men wish to be wise and happy? For I do not doubt at all that you see it, and that it is true. Do you see this then as your own thought in such wise that if you did not tell me I should be completely ignorant of it, or so that you may understand it, and this truth may be seen by me even though you have not told it to me?

E. Nay, I do not doubt that it can also be seen by you, even were I unwilling.

A. But then if we both see one truth with our individual minds, is not that truth common to both of us?

E. Evidently.

A. Again, I believe you do not deny that wisdom should be sought after, and concede that this is true?

E. I do not question that at all.

A. Can we then deny that this is likewise true, and one, and to be seen in common by all who know it; although each one sees it, not with my mind nor with yours, nor with the mind of any other, but with his own mind; while what he sees is there for all to see in common?

E. Surely not.

A. Again—We should live justly, put worse things below better, and compare equal things with equal, and give to each man what is properly his: do you not acknowledge this to be most true, and to be present in common to me and to all who see it, as well as to you?

E. I agree.

A. Can you deny that an uncorrupted thing is better than a corrupted thing, an eternal thing than a temporal thing, an inviolable than a violable?

E. Who can deny it?

A. Can anyone then call this truth his private possession, when it is changelessly present for the contemplation of all who are able to contemplate it?

E. No one can truly say that it is his exclusively, since it is as much one and common to all as it is true.

A. Again, who denies that the soul should be turned away from corruption and toward incorruption; that is, that not corruption, but incorruption should be loved? Or who, when he acknowledges that this is true, does not also understand it to be immutable and see that it stands there for all minds in common that are able to contemplate it?

E. Most true.

A. And does anyone doubt that that life which can be shaken by no adversity in its true and honest opinions is better than that which is easily ruined and broken by transient misfortune?

E. Who would doubt that?

29. *A.* I will ask no more questions of this sort now; for it is enough that you see as well as I, and concede it to be most certain, that these rules, and as it were lights of virtue, are true and immutable, and singly or all together are present for the common contemplation of those who, each with his own mind and reason, are able to perceive them. But I do ask whether you think that these rules pertain to wisdom? For I believe that he who has attained wisdom will seem wise to you.

E. He certainly will.

A. Well, could he who lives justly so live if he did not see what lower things to subordinate to what higher, and what equal things to join to each other, and how to distribute to each what is properly his own?

E. He could not.

A. Will you then deny that he who sees this sees wisely?

E. I do not deny it.

A. And does not he who lives prudently choose incorruption, and see that it is to be preferred to corruption?

E. Clearly so.

A. When, therefore, he chooses that which no one doubts should be chosen as the object toward which he should turn his soul, can it be denied that he chooses wisely?

E. I should certainly not deny it.

A. Therefore, when he turns his soul to that which he chooses wisely, he turns his soul wisely.

E. Surely.

A. And he who is not driven away by any fears or penalties from that to which he wisely turns himself, without doubt acts wisely.

E. Without doubt indeed.

A. It is very clear, therefore, that all these things, which we have called rules and lights of the virtues, pertain to wisdom; inasmuch as the more one uses them in the conduct of life, and lives his life according to them, the more he lives and acts wisely. But what is done wisely cannot rightly be said to be separated from wisdom.

E. Just so.

A. Just as, therefore, there are true and immutable rules of numbers, the reason and truth of which you have said is immutably present to all perceivers in common; so there are true and immutable rules of wisdom, concerning a few of which, when you were just now asked about them one by one, you answered that they were true and manifest, and conceded that they are present for the common contemplation of all who are able to regard them.

CHAPTER XI

Whether wisdom and number are the same, or whether one arises from the other, or exists in the other.

30. *E.* I cannot doubt it. But I would much like to know whether these two, wisdom and number, are contained in some one

genus, as you have mentioned that they are also joined together in the holy Scriptures; or whether one arises from the other, or consists in the other, as number from wisdom, or in wisdom. For I should not have ventured to say that wisdom arises from number, or consists in number, for I know not how this could be; for wisdom strikes me as far more venerable than number, because I have known many calculators or computers, or whatever else you may call them, who reckon superbly and marvellously—but of wise men only a very few or possibly none.

A. You say something at which I too often wonder. For when I reflect upon the immutable truth of numbers, and upon its lair as it were, or shrine, or region, or whatever else we may appropriately call the dwelling place and seat as it were of numbers, I am far removed from the body; and finding maybe something which I can think, but not finding anything which I can put into words, I return as if wearied to this world of ours, so that I may speak, and may talk of those things that are not set before our eyes as they are wont to be talked of. This happens to me too, when as best I can I think very carefully and intently about wisdom. And because of this I wonder much, since these two are in the most mysterious and certain truth, and the testimony of the Scriptures is added also, in which, as I have noted, they are placed together—I wonder greatly, as I have said, why to the multitude of men number is held of small account and wisdom dear.

But doubtless it is this, that there is one, and as it were the same thing; but yet, since it is none the less said of wisdom in the divine Books that it *reaches from the end unto the end mightily, and disposes all things sweetly,** that power by which it *reaches from the end unto the end mightily* is perhaps called number, but that which *disposes all things sweetly* is wisdom strictly so called; while both are of one and the same wisdom.

---

*Wisdom, VIII, 1.

31.　But because God gave numbers to all things, even to the lowest, and to those placed in the end of things—for all bodies though they are among things the meanest, have their numbers—yet to be wise He did not grant to bodies, or even to all souls, but only to rational souls, as if He placed in them a seat for Himself, from which He disposes all those lowest things to which He gave numbers. And so since we judge easily of numbers, as of the things which are ordered beneath us, on which we perceived the impressed numbers as beneath us, we therefore hold them also of less account. But when we begin to turn back, and as it were upwards, we find that they too transcend our minds, and remain immutable in truth itself. And because few can be wise, whereas to count is granted even to fools, men admire wisdom and despise numbers. The learned however, and the studious, the more remote they are from earthly blemish, the more they look upon both number and wisdom in truth itself, and hold both dear; and in comparison with its truth, not for them are gold and silver, and other things for which men contend, but even their own selves grow unimportant.

32.　Nor should you wonder that numbers are held cheap by men, and wisdom dear, because they can more easily count than be wise; when you see them hold gold dearer than the light of a lamp, and laugh to see gold compared with it. But a far inferior thing is honored, because even a beggar lights himself a lamp, but few have gold: although wisdom may be lacking, so that in comparison with number it is found inferior, while it is the same, but seeks the eye by which it can be seen.*

But just as brightness and heat are perceived consubstantial, so to speak, in one fire, and yet the heat reaches only those things that are brought close, while the brightness is diffused farther and more widely; in like manner by the power of

---

quamquam sapientia absit ut in comparatione numeri inveniatur inferior, cum eadem sit, sed oculum quo cerni possit, inquiris. This passage is obscure. The English is essentially the same as McKeon's version.

understanding that is present in wisdom the nearer things, such as the rational souls, grow warm, but the more remote things, such as bodies, are not reached by the heat of being wise, but are suffused by the light of numbers. This is perhaps obscure to you; for no visible thing can be made a perfect analogy of something invisible. Only note this, which is enough for the question in hand, and which reveals itself even to humbler minds like ours; that even if it cannot be clear to us whether number is in wisdom or from wisdom, or wisdom itself is in number or from number, or whether it can be shown that they are names for one thing; it is certainly manifest that both are true, and true immutably.

CHAPTER XII

There is a single immutable truth in all understandings, and it is superior to our minds.

33.   Wherefore you will certainly not deny that there is an immutable truth, containing all things that are immutably true, which you cannot say is yours or mine or any one man's; but that in some wonderful way a mysterious and universal light, as it were, is present and proffers itself to all in common. But who would say that that which is commonly present to all who reason and understand belongs properly to the nature of any one of them? For you remember, I think, what we said a little while ago about the bodily senses; namely, that those things which we perceive in common by the sense of the eyes or ears, such as colors and sounds, do not pertain to the nature of our eyes or ears, but are there for all to perceive in common. So too it will not do for you to say that those things which we see in common, each with his own mind, pertain to the nature of the mind of either one of us. For what the eyes of two persons see at the same time, cannot be said to be the eyes of this man or of that, but is some third thing to which the gaze of both is turned.

E. That is manifestly true.

34. *A.* Do you think then that this truth, which we have been discussing at such length, and in which, single though it be, we have discerned so many things, is more excellent than our minds, or equal to them, or is it even inferior?

But if it were inferior we would judge not according to it, but concerning it; just as we judge of bodies because they are below us, and say commonly not only that they are so or not so, but that they ought to be so or not so. So too of our minds we know not only that the mind is so, but frequently also that it should be so. And of bodies to be sure we judge thus when we say: this is not as white as it should be, or not as square, and many similar things. But of minds: it is less apt than it should be, or less gentle, or less vehement; according as the manner of our character shows itself. And we judge of these things according to those inner rules of truth that we discern in common; but no one judges in any way of the rules themselves. For when anyone says that eternal things are better than temporal, or that seven and three are ten, no one says that it ought to be so; but knowing that it is so, he does not correct it as an examiner, but rejoices in it as a discoverer.

If again the truth were equal to our minds, it would be also mutable. For our minds perceive it sometimes more and sometimes less, and thereby acknowledge themselves mutable, while it, continuing in itself, is neither enhanced when we see it more, nor diminished when we see it less, but whole and uncorrupted it makes glad those who turn to it, and punishes with blindness those who turn away. But what then, if also we judge of those same minds according to that truth, while we can in no way judge of it? For we say of our mind: it understands less than it should or it understands as much as it should. But a mind should understand in the measure that it is able to draw near to and cleave to immutable truth. Wherefore, if that truth be neither inferior nor equal to our minds, it remains that it is higher and more excellent.

CHAPTER XIII

Exhortation to embrace truth, which alone makes men happy.

35.   I promised however, as you will remember, that I would show you something more sublime than our mind and reason. Behold, it is truth! Embrace it if you can, and enjoy it, and delight in the Lord, and He will give you the desires of your heart.* For what do you desire more than to be happy? And who is so happy as he who enjoys truth—unshaken, and immutable, and also excellent?

Do men, forsooth, proclaim themselves happy, when lusting with great desire they embrace the fair bodies of wives, or even harlots: and shall we doubt that we are happy in the embrace of truth?

Men proclaim themselves happy, when with heat-parched throats they reach a pure and abundant spring; or famished, find an elaborate and bountiful repast: and will we deny that we are happy who are watered and fed by truth?

We are wont to hear the voices of those who proclaim themselves happy, when they lie among roses and other flowers, or even if they enjoy sweet-smelling unguents: but what is more fragrant, more delicious, than the inspiration of truth? And do we hesitate when we are inspired by it to call ourselves happy?

Many make for themselves a happy life in the song of voices, and of strings and flutes; and when these are wanting they deem themselves miserable, but when they are present they are transported by joy: and when without, so to speak, any din of songs, a kind of eloquent silence of truth steals upon our minds, shall we seek another happy life, and not enjoy the one so instant and so sure?

Men who love the gleam of gold and silver, the sparkle of gems or bright colors, or the clarity and pleasantness of the light itself that reaches these eyes—be it in earthly fires, or

---

*Psalm XXXVII, 4.

stars, or moon, or sun—think themselves happy when they are not recalled from that pleasure by any vexation or need, and for these would fain live always: and do we fear to place a happy life in the light of truth?

36. Yea, truly, since in truth the supreme good is perceived and held secure, and that truth is wisdom, let us descry the supreme good in it, and grasp it and enjoy it. For he is indeed happy who enjoys the supreme good. For this truth spreads before us all those goods that singly or together men of understanding, each to the measure of his grasp, choose for themselves and enjoy. But just as men in the light of the sun choose that which they would fain gaze upon, and are gladdened by the sight; whereas if there were perchance any of more robust health and endowed with stronger eyes, these would look upon nothing more willingly than the sun itself, which lights up also all those other things that delight weaker eyes: so the keen vision of a strong and active mind, when with sure reason it has looked upon many things true and unchanging, turns toward truth itself, through which all things are made evident; and cleaving, as it were, to that truth, forgets all things else, and in it at once enjoys them all. For whatever is pleasant in other truths is surely present in truth itself.

37. This is our freedom, when we are submissive to that truth; and it itself is our God, who frees us from death, that is from the state of sin. For Truth itself, speaking as man to men, has said to those who believe in Him: *If ye continue in my word, then are ye my disciples indeed; and ye shall know the truth, and the truth shall make you free.** For the soul enjoys no thing with freedom, except that which it enjoys with security.

---

*John, VIII, 31, 32.

CHAPTER XIV

Truth is possessed with security.

But no one is secure in those things which he can lose against his will. No one unwilling, however, loses truth and wisdom. For one cannot be separated from it by occasions, but what is called separation from truth and wisdom is a perverse will, by which inferior things are chosen; but no one wills anything unwillingly. We have therefore that which all may enjoy in common; there are no difficulties and no defects in it. It takes to itself all lovers, with none the least envious, and is common to all and chaste to each. No one says to another: Move back, that I too may draw near; remove your hands, that I too may embrace. All cling to it; all touch the thing itself. No portion of its food is torn away; you drink naught of it that I cannot drink: for by that common participation in it you do not convert anything to your private possession; but what you take from it remains whole for me. I do not wait for what inspired by it; for naught of it is at any time made the property of any one, or of a few, but the whole is at one time common to all.

38.   Less like this truth therefore are those things that we touch or taste or smell, and more like it those that we see and hear; because every word is heard entire by all those by whom it is heard, and heard entire by each at the same time, and every visible object that is before the eyes is seen at the same time as much by one as by another. But even these are like it at a great remove; for not all of any voice sounds at one time, but some of it sounds earlier and some later; and every visible object swells out, so to speak, through space, and is not everywhere whole. And assuredly all of these are taken from us despite our will, and difficulties of one sort or another stand in the way of our enjoying them. For even if the sweet singing of someone should last forever, and people vied with one another to listen to it, they would crowd together and fight for places, there would be such a multitude, that each might

be nearer the singer; and in hearing they would hold nothing that would remain with them, but would be touched by sounds that all vanish. Moreover, if I wished to look at the sun, and could do so persistently, it would desert me in its setting, or when veiled by a cloud, and by many other obstacles would I lose unwillingly the pleasure of seeing it. Finally, even were this sweetness of seeing light and hearing voices ever present to me, it were no great thing, seeing that it would be common to me and to the brutes. But the beauty of truth and wisdom, so long as there is a steadfast will to enjoy it, does not shut off comers by the thronged multitude of listeners, nor does it play through time, nor wander to places, nor is it interrupted by night or shut off by shadows, nor is it subject to the senses of the body. To those who from the whole world have turned to it for their delight, it is very near to all, to all everlasting; it is in no place, it is never away; it admonishes openly; it teaches inwardly; it changes all who see it to better, by none is it changed to worse; no one judges of it, without it no one judges well. And from this it is manifest beyond doubt that it is superior to our minds, which are each made wise by it; and of it you may not judge, but through it you may judge all things else.

CHAPTER XV

That God exists is shown fully by reason, and is now certainly known.

39.   You conceded, however, that if I should show you something higher than our minds, you would confess that it is God, if there were nothing yet higher. Accepting this concession of yours I said that it would be enough if I should prove this. For if there is something yet more excellent than truth, that rather is God; but if not, then truth itself is God. Whether therefore there is this more excellent thing, or whether there is not, you cannot deny that God is, which was the question set for our discussion and treatment. For if you

are disturbed by what we have received in faith from the sacred teaching of Christ, that God is the Father of Wisdom, remember that we have also accepted in faith that equal to the eternal Father is the Wisdom begotten of Him. Wherefore nothing more need be asked, but only held with steadfast faith. For God is; and He is truly and supremely. This, I think, we not only hold now undoubted by faith, but know also by a sure, albeit still rather tenuous form of knowledge; which for the question in hand is enough to explain the other things that pertain to the matter. Unless, that is, you have something to say in objection.

E. Nay, I accept these things, and am completely filled with an incredible joy, which I cannot express in words, and I cry out that they are most sure. I cry out moreover with an inner voice by which I wish to be heard by truth itself, and to cleave to it; because I concede it to be not only good, but the supreme good and the maker of happiness.

A. Rightly so: and I too rejoice greatly. But I would ask whether we are now wise and happy, or whether we as yet only incline that way, so that it may come forth and be ours?

E. I think rather that we incline to it.

A. Whence then do you understand thse things, at whose certainty and truth you cried out that you rejoiced? And do you grant that they pertain to wisdom? Or is any fool able to know wisdom?

E. So long as he is a fool he cannot.

A. You, then, are wise; or else you do not know wisdom.

E. I am certainly not yet wise, but neither would I call myself a fool in so far as I know wisdom; since these things which I know are certain, and I cannot deny that they pertain to wisdom.

A. Tell me, pray, will you not admit that he who is not just is unjust, and he who is not prudent is imprudent, and he who is not temperate is intemperate? Can there be any doubt as to this?

E. I admit that when a man is not just he is unjust; and

would give the same reply as to the prudent and temperate man.

A. Why, then, when he is not wise, is he not foolish?

E. I admit that too: when one is not wise, he is a fool.

A. Well then, which of these are you?

E. Whichever you call me; I should not dare to call myself wise, and I see that it follows from those things that I conceded, that I should not hesitate to say I am a fool.

A. Therefore the fool knows wisdom. For he would not be sure, as we said just now is the case, that he wished to be wise, and that he ought to wish it, if there were not inherent in his mind a notion of wisdom as having to do with those matters, concerning which you answered when asked about them separately, and which pertain to wisdom, and in the knowledge of which you rejoiced.

E. It is as you say.

CHAPTER XVI

To those who seek her earnestly, wisdom shows herself along the way; namely, by numbers impressed on each thing.

41. *A.* What else therefore do we do when we study to be wise, except to concentrate our whole soul with all the ardor we can upon what we touch with our mind, and as it were place it there and fix it unshakeably; so that it may no longer enjoy privately what has entangled it in passing things, but freed from all influence of times or places may lay hold on that which is ever one and the same. For just as the soul is the whole life of the body, the happy life of the soul is God. While we do this, and until we have completed it, we are on the way.

And it is granted to us to rejoice in these true and sure goods, albeit they are as yet but flickering lights on this dark road. For is not this what is written about wisdom, when we are told how she deals with her lovers when they come to her: *She showeth herself joyfully to them along the ways,*

*and runneth to meet them with all providence.** For whither-
soever you turn, by certain marks imprinted on her works she
speaks to you, and when you slip back into eternal things,
she again calls you within by the very forms of those things
outside; so that you see that whatever delights you in the
body, or allures through the bodily senses, is numbered. And
you ask why this is, and return within yourself and understand that you cannot approve or find fault with that which
you touch with your bodily senses, unless you have at hand
certain laws of beauty, to which you may refer whatever
beautiful things you may perceive externally.

42.   Look on earth and sky and sea, and whatsoever things are
in them, or shine from above, or creep beneath, or fly, or
swim; they have forms because they have numbers: take these
away, they will be nothing. From what then are they, if not
from number; seeing that they have being only in so far as
they have number?

And even human artificers, makers of all corporeal forms,
have numbers in their art to which they fit their works: and
they move hands and tools in the fashioning till that which
is formed outside, carried back to the light of numbers which
is within, so far as may be attains perfection, and through
the mediating sense pleases the inner judge looking upon the
heavenly numbers.

Then seek what moves the limbs of the artificer himself: it
will be number; for they too are moved in the rhythm of
numbers. And if you take away the work from the hands,
and from the mind the intention of making something, and
that motion is directed toward pleasure, you will have a dance.
Seek then what it is that gives pleasure in a dance: number
will answer, "Behold, it is I."

Look now upon the beauty of the formed body; numbers
are held in space. Examine the beauty of mobility in the body;
numbers move around in time. Go into the art whence these

---

*Wisdom, VI, 17.

proceed, seek in it time and place: never will it be, nowhere will it be; yet number lives in it, nor is its region of spaces, nor its age of days; and yet when they who would be artists apply themselves to learning the art, they move their bodies through space and time, and even their mind through time— with the passing of time, to be sure, they become more skilful. Transcend, therefore, the artist's mind also, to see the sempiternal number. Now wisdom will flash forth to you from her innermost throne, and from the very sanctuary of truth. If she dazzles and blinds your as yet too feeble vision, turn back the eye of the mind into that path where she showed herself joyfully; but remember then that you have put off the vision which when you are stronger and sounder you may seek again.

43.   Alas for them that forsake your guidance, and stray from your footsteps, who love your signs in your stead, and forget what you are signing to them, O Wisdom, sweetest light of the cleansed mind! For you do not cease to sign to us who you are, and how great; and your signs are all the ornament of created things. For the artist too in a way makes signs to one who views his work, not to be wholly absorbed in the beauty of the work itself, but so to run his eye over the appearance of the fabricated body that he may turn back with love to him who made it. But they who love in your stead the things you do are like men who listen to some wise speech, who attend too eagerly to the sweetness of the voice and the cadence of neatly turned phrases, and miss the loftiness of the thoughts of which the sounds of the words are but signs. Alas for them that turn away from your light, and cling to the ease of their own darkness! For as if turning their backs on you, they are fixed in carnal works even as in their own shadows, notwithstanding that what delights them even there they have by virtue of the circumfulgence of your light. But while they love the shade, it makes dull the eye of the soul, and too weak to bear the sight of you. Therefore a man is more and more in darkness, the more ready he is to pursue something which receives more indulgently the weaker (light). From this he

begins to lose the power to see that which supremely is, and to think evil whatever fails him for want of foresight, or leads him astray when he desires it, or torments him when it lays hold on him; when in fact he deservedly suffers these things for turning away from wisdom: and whatever is just cannot be evil.

44.   If therefore you cannot lay hold on anything, either by the sense of the body or by considering it with the mind, unless it is held in some form of numbers, and falls back again into nothingness when this is taken away; be assured that there exists some eternal and immutable form, so that these mutable things are not cut short, but in their measured movements and the distinct variety of their forms, go through as it were the measures of a dance; and this form is neither contained, and so to speak spread through space, nor has it duration and change with time, but through it all those other things have power to take shape, and according to their kind to fill and to run through the numbers of places and times.

CHAPTER XVII

Every good and perfection whatsoever is from God.

45.   For everything changeable is of necessity also formable. But as we say a thing is changeable when it can be changed, so we should call formable that which can be formed. No thing, moreover, can form itself; because no thing can give itself that which it has not, and surely anything that is formed is given a form. Wherefore if a thing has some form it has no need to receive that which it has already, but if it has no form it cannot receive from itself what it has not. Therefore, as we have said, no thing can form itself.

But what more can we say of the mutability of body and mind! For enough has been said already. And so it follows that both body and mind are informed by a certain changeless and ever-continuing form. Of which form it is said: *Thou shalt change them and they shall be changed, but thou art the* *same, and thy years shall have no end.** The prophetic language used *years without end* for eternity. Of this same form it is likewise said that *continuing in itself it renews all things.*† From this it is understood also that all things are governed by Providence. For if all things that are would be naught, if completely deprived of form, that immutable form through which all mutable things subsist, that they may be filled and moved by the numbers of their forms, is itself their providence; for they would not be, if it were not. Whosoever therefore, regarding and considering the whole of creation, keeps the road to wisdom, sees wisdom show herself joyfully to him along the ways, and run to meet him with all providence; and he burns the more eagerly to complete that journey, the more the way is made beautiful by her whom he is on fire to reach.

46.   But only if you can find some other kind of created thing besides that which is, but does not live, and that which is and lives, but does not understand, and that which is and lives and understands, can you venture to say that there is some good which is not from God. We can moreover express these three by two names if we call them body and life; because that which lives only, but does not understand, such as the life of beasts, and that which understands, such as the life of man, are both rightly called life. But these two, body and life, are certainly to be classed as creatures (for the life of the Creator is spoken of too; and that is the supreme life). These two creatures therefore, since they are formable, as earlier remarks have shown, and fall back into nothing if form be utterly lost, show clearly enough that they subsist from that form which is ever such. Wherefore all goods, whatever their degree, be they great or be they small, cannot be except from God.

For what in creatures can be greater than an understanding life, and what can be less than body? Howsoever much they

---

*Psalm CII, 26, 27.
†Wisdom, VII, 27.

are wanting, and tend thereby not to be, something neverthless of form remains to them, that in some way they may exist. But whatever of form remains to any deficient thing is from that form which knows no deficiency, and does not suffer the movements themselves of things deficient or efficient to go beyond the laws of their numbers. Therefore anything praiseworthy that is noted in the nature of things, be it judged worthy of slight praise or of great, must be referred to the most excellent and ineffable praise of the Creator: unless you have something to say against all this.

CHAPTER XVIII

Free will, even though it can be turned to a bad use, is to be counted among goods.

47. E. I admit that I am convinced sufficiently, and to the extent that it can be made clear in this life and among such as we, that God is, and that all goods are from God; since all things that are, whether they are those that are, and live, and understand, or those which only are and live, or those which only are, are from God. But now let us look at the third question: whether it can be established that free will is to be numbered among goods. If this is proved, I shall concede without hesitation that God gave it to us, and that it should have been given.

A. You have remembered well what was proposed, and have been alert enough to see that the second question is now explained. But you should have seen that the third question also is now answered.

For you said indeed that it seemed to you that free choice of will ought not to have been given, because by it one sins. When against this view of yours I objected that it was not possible to do rightly except by free choice of will, and asserted that God had given it rather for this purpose; you answered that free will should have been given in the way justice, which no one can use except rightly, was given. This answer of yours forced us to make all those digressions in the argument, whereby we proved to you that there were no goods, great or small, that were not from God. This could not be shown with sufficient clearness, unless, in opposing the opinions of impious folly whereby the fool says in his heart there is no God, whatever reasoning our small abilities could bring to bear on so great a matter—that same God helping us in a road so perilous—should take its start from something self-evident. But these two things, namely, that God is, and that all goods are from Him, which even previously were held with unshaken faith, were nevertheless discussed in such a manner that also this third thing, that free will is to be counted among goods, might stand out in clearest light.

48.   For it was revealed by our earlier discussion, and agreed, that the nature of body is on a lower stage than the nature of soul, and that therefore soul is a greater good than body. If therefore we find among the goods of the body some which man may use not rightly, and which notwithstanding we cannot say should not have been given, since we acknowledge them to be goods; what wonder is it if also in the soul there are certain goods which too we may not use rightly, but which, being goods, could have been given only by Him from whom all good things are?

But you see how great a good is lacking to a body which lacks hands; and yet he uses his hands for ill who works with them shameful or violent deeds. If you should see anyone without feet, you would acknowledge that a very great good was wanting to the wholeness of his body; and yet you would not deny that he who should use his feet to harm another or to dishonor himself would be using his feet wrongfully. With our eyes we see this light, and distinguish the shapes of bodies. Being moreover the most beautiful thing in our body, these organs are placed, so to speak, at the summit of dignity, and they serve to guard our safety and many other useful purposes. Nevertheless, most men do many base things with their eyes, and force them to fight on the side of lust.

And you see too how great a good is wanting in a face that has no eyes. But when they are there who has given us these but God, the generous giver of all goods? Just as, therefore, you approve these things in the body, and not regarding those who use them for ill praise Him who has given these goods; you should in like manner acknowledge that free will, without which no one can live rightly, is a good thing, and given by God; and should think that they are to be condemned who use this good for ill, rather than that He who gave it should not have given it.

49. *E.* I should like you then to first prove to me that free will is a good thing. I will then concede that God gave it, because I acknowledge that all goods are from God.

A. So, then, have I not proved it to you by all the effort of our former argument, when you acknowledged that every species and form of body subsists in the supreme form of all things, that is, in the truth, and conceded this to be a good? For even the hairs of our head are numbered, as Truth himself says in the Gospel.* Has it slipped your mind what we said about the supremacy of number, and its power of reaching from the end even to the end? But what perversity is that! The hairs of our head, notwithstanding that they are the smallest and lowliest of things, are to be counted among the goods; nor can they be ascribed to any author save God the creator of all good things, because the greatest and least of goods are from Him from whom is every good; and you are in doubt as to free will, without which even they who lead the worst of lives concede that they could not live rightly.

So pray tell me truly, which in us do you think better: that without which we can live rightly, or that without which we cannot live rightly?

E. No more, I beg you! I am ashamed of my blindness. For who doubts that that is more excellent by far, without which no life is upright?

---

*Matt. X, 30.

A. You will not deny then that a blind man can live rightly?

E. Far from me be such folly.

A. Since, therefore, you grant that in the body the eye is a good, although its loss does not prevent us from living rightly; will free will, without which no one can live rightly, seem no good thing to you?

50.   You look upon justice, which no one uses for ill. This is counted among the highest goods in man himself, and among all those virtues of the soul upon which an upright and honorable life is based. For no one uses prudence, or fortitude, or temperance for ill; for in all these, as in justice which you mentioned, right reason is active, without which there can be no virtue. But no one uses right reason wrongly.

CHAPTER XIX

Great, small, and intermediate goods. Freedom is numbered among the intermediate.

These therefore are great goods. But you must remember that not only the great goods, but also the smallest, could not be except from Him from whom are all goods; that is, from God. For that was shown by the earliest argument, to which you agreed so often and so gladly. The virtues by which we live rightly are therefore great goods: the forms of bodies of any kind, since we can live rightly without them, are the smallest goods. But the powers of the soul, without which we cannot live rightly, are in fact intermediate goods. For no one makes a bad use of the virtues; but the other goods, that is the small and intermediate, can be used by anyone not only for good, but also for evil. And no one uses a virtue for evil, because the action of a virtue is in the good use of those things which we can also use wrongly; but no one uses it wrongly by a right use. Whereby the abundance and greatness of God's goodness is responsible for the existence not only of the great goods, but also of the lesser and intermediate goods. His goodness is more to be praised in the great than in the middle goods, and more in the middle than the lesser; but more in all than if He had not bestowed all.

51. *E.* I agree. But one thing bothers me: since we are discussing free will, and see that it itself uses things well or badly, how can it too be counted among the things we use?

A. Just as we perceive by reason all things which we perceive and know, and reason nevertheless is counted among the things we perceive by reason. Have you forgotten that when we were inquiring what things were known by reason, you conceded that reason too is known by reason? Do not wonder then, that if we use other things by our free will, we can also use that free will by the will itself; so that in some fashion the will which uses other things uses itself, just as the reason which perceives other things perceives also itself. For memory too holds in its grasp not only all those other things that we remember, but also, since we do not forget that we have a memory, it holds itself in us in some fashion; or rather we remember ourselves, and other things, and our memory, through memory itself.

52. Therefore when the will, which is a middle good, cleaves to a good which is immutable, and not personal, but universal —such as is that truth about which we have said much, though nothing worthy of it—man holds secure a happy life; and that happy life, that is, the disposition of the soul cleaving to the immutable good, is man's peculiar and highest good. In that good are also all virtues, which no one can use for ill. For though these are great and chief goods in man, it is none the less quite clear that they are not common, but are proper to each individual man. But by truth and wisdom, which are common to all, all are made wise and happy who cling to them. But one man is not made happy by the happiness of another man, because even when he seeks to be happy by imitating the other, he seeks to be made happy by that which has made the other happy, that is by immutable and universal truth. Nor does the prudence of one make another

prudent, nor the fortitude of one make another strong, nor his temperance make another temperate; nor is anyone made just by the justice of another: but the second must bring his soul into accord with those immutable rules and lights of virtue, with which the one endowed with the virtues, whom the other proposes to imitate, has fixed his soul and brought it into accord.[1]

53.   The will therefore that cleaves to the universal and immutable good obtains the great and chief goods of man, while it itself is one of the middle goods. But the will that is turned away from the universal and immutable good, and turned towards personal goods, or towards something external, or something lower, sins. It is turned towards personal goods when it desires to be self-sufficing; towards external things when it is busied with knowing the private affairs of others, or whatever is not its own affair; towards lower things when it loves bodily delights: and so the proud man, and the inquisitive, and the lascivious, are caught up in another life which in comparison to the higher life is death—a life which nevertheless is ruled by the administration of divine Providence, which orders all things in their fitting places, and which distributes his own to each according to his deserts. And so it is that those goods which are sought by sinful men are not in any way bad, nor is the will itself, which we have found to be numbered among the goods; but the evil is its turning away from the immutable good and turning towards mutable goods: which aversion and adversion are nevertheless not forced, but voluntary, and therefore are followed by the meet and just punishment of wretchedness.

---

[1] But by adjusting his mind to those unchangeable rules and lights of the virtues which live incorruptibly in truth itself and in the common wisdom to which he (the ideal man) has set and adapted his mind, (and) which indeed, endowed with those virtues, he has set before himself to imitate. M.

CHAPTER XX

That movement, by which the will is turned away from immutable good, is not from God.

54.   But since the will is moved when it turns itself from the immutable to a mutable good, you will perhaps want to know whence arises this movement, which assuredly is bad, even though the free will is to be counted among goods, since without it there can be no right living. For if that movement, that is the turning away of the will from the Lord God, is without doubt a sin, can we say that God is the author of sin? Therefore the movement is not from God. Whence then is it?

If I should answer your question by saying that I do not know, you will perhaps be disappointed; but I should neverthe less be answering truly. For what is nothing cannot be known. Keep your piety so unshaken that no good occurs to you that is not from God; whether you perceive it, or understand it, or in any way think of it. For so no nature will occur to you that is not from God. Do not hesitate to ascribe to God indeed everything where you see measure, and number, and order. But when you take these away utterly, nothing at all will remain. Because even should there remain some rudiment of form where you may find neither measure, nor number, nor order (because wherever these are the form is perfected) you should take away even that rudiment of form, which appears as it were as material awaiting the hand of the artist for its perfection; for if good is the perfection of form, even the rudiment of form will be some good. So when all good is taken utterly away, there will remain, not something surely, but absolutely nothing.

But every good is from God; there is therefore no nature that is not from God. But since that movement of turning away, which we acknowledge sin to be, is a movement of ceasing, and every ceasing comes from nothing, see to what that pertains, and do not doubt that it does not pertain to God. This ceasing nevertheless, since it is voluntary, is placed in our power. For if you fear it, it must be that you do not will it; but if you do not will it, it will not be. What then is safer than to be in that life where what you do not will cannot befall you? But since man cannot rise of his own accord, in the same way that he fell of his own accord, the right hand of God is held out to us from on high: that is to say, let us hold in steadfast faith our Lord Jesus Christ, and await Him in certain hope, and long for Him with a burning love.

But if you think that there is anything about the origin of sins that demands more careful inquiry (for I do not see any need whatever)—but if you still think so, we must put it off for another discussion.

E. I accede to your wish, to be sure, that we postpone to another time what pertains to this matter. For I do not concur in your opinion that it has already been sufficiently investigated.

BOOK THREE

WHEREIN IT IS ASKED WHENCE ARISES THAT MOVEMENT BY WHICH THE WILL IS TURNED AWAY FROM IMMUTABLE GOOD. DO GOD'S FOREKNOWLEDGE OF THE SINS OF MEN, AND THE FREEDOM OF MEN THEMSELVES TO SIN CONFLICT WITH ONE ANOTHER? IT IS PRESENTLY SHOWN THAT THE CREATOR IS NOWISE AT FAULT FOR WHAT SO HAPPENS BY NECESSITY IN THE CREATURE THAT IT IS DONE BY THE WILL OF SINNERS; AND THAT FOR THE PROLONGING AND PUNISHMENT OF CREATURES WHO ARE LIABLE TO SIN GOD IS WHOLY TO BE PRAISED. THE ARGUMENT THEN LEADING TO THE SUBJECT OF ORIGINAL SIN, IT IS MADE CLEAR WHEREFORE IT CONTINUES NOT AT ALL UNJUSTLY IN THE DESCENDANTS OF ADAM, AND THAT SINNERS UNDESERVINGLY PLEAD THIS AS AN EXCUSE. FINALLY, SOME DIFFICULTIES CONNECTED WITH THIS ARE UNRAVELED.

CHAPTER I

Whence that movement is, by which the will is turned away from the immutable good.

1. *E.* Since it is clear enough to me that free will is to be numbered among the goods, and indeed not among the least, and that we are thence forced to acknowledge that it was given by God, and that it ought to have been given; now, if you think it a suitable occasion, I should like to know from you whence arises that movement by which the will is turned away from universal and immutable good, and turned toward personal, or alien, or low goods—all mutable.

A. What need to know that?

E. Because if free will has been so given that that movement is natural to it, then it turns toward these things by necessity; and so no fault can be found where nature and necessity rule.

A. Does this movement please you, or does it displease you?

E. It displeases me.

A. Then you reprehend it.

E. Certainly I reprehend it.

A. You reprehend, therefore, a blameless movement of the soul.

E. I do not reprehend a blameless movement of the soul, but I do not know that it is a fault, to leave the immutable good and turn to mutable goods.

A. Then you reprehend what you do not know.

E. Do not twist my words. For I said, "I do not *know*," so as to have it understood that without doubt there is a fault. For by the way I said, "I do not *know*," I was really ridiculing any doubt about a matter so manifest.

A. What surest truth is this, that has made you forget what you said a little while ago? For if that movement arises by nature or necessity it could not possibly be culpable; but you so firmly believe it to be culpable, that you think ridiculous any doubt about a thing so certain. Why then do you think to assert, or at any rate to consider as possibly true, something that you yourself prove to be patently false? For you said that if free will is so given that it has that movement by nature, then it turns toward those things by necessity; so that no fault can be found where nature and necessity rule. But you should have no doubt whatever that it was not so given, when you do not doubt that the movement is culpable.

E. I myself said that the movement is culpable, and on that account it displeases me, and I cannot doubt that it is to be reprehended. But I deny that the soul is to be blamed which is drawn away from the immutable good to mutable goods, if its nature is such that it is moved thereto by necessity.

2. *A.* Whose is that movement, which you grant is surely to be blamed?

E. I see it in the soul, but whose it is I do not know.

A. Do you deny that the soul is moved by that movement?

E. I do not deny it.

A. Do you deny then that the movement by which a stone is moved is the stone's movement? For I am not speaking of that movement by which we move it, or when it is moved by an outside force, as when it is thrown into the air, but of the movement by which it turns and falls to the earth by its own gravity.

E. To be sure I do not deny that the movement by which it tends downward, as you say, and seeks the lowest place, is the stone's movement, but it is natural. If moreover the soul too has that movement in this manner, surely it too is natural, and since it is moved naturally cannot rightly be reproached; because even if it be moved to its ruin, it is driven thereto by the necessity of its nature. Furthermore, since we do not doubt that the movement is culpable, we must deny altogether that it is natural; and therefore it is not like that movement by which the stone is moved naturally.

A. Did we establish anything by our two former discussions?

E. Surely we did.

A. I believe you will remember then that it was pretty clearly shown in the first discussion that the mind is made the slave of lust only by its own will; for it cannot be forced to this shame either by a superior or an equal, because that is unjust, nor by an inferior, because he has not the power. We can only conclude, therefore, that this movement, by which the will to enjoy is turned from the Creator to the creature, is its own. If this movement is to be accounted a fault (and you think anyone doubting this deserving of ridicule) it is certainly not natural, but voluntary. It is like the movement by which the stone is borne downward in that it is proper to it, just as that movement was proper to the stone. But it is nevertheless unlike it in this respect: that the stone does not have it in its power to restrain the movement by which it is borne downward; whereas the soul, so long as it does not will it, is not moved to forsake the higher things and choose the lower; so that the movement of the stone is natural, whereas that of the soul is voluntary. That is why, if anyone should say that the stone sins, because it tends downward of its own weight, I would say, not that he has less sense than the stone itself, but that he should certainly be judged mad; whereas we convict the soul of sin when we prove that it prefers to leave higher things and enjoy lower. What need therefore to inquire whence arises this movement, by which the soul is turned away from immutable good and towards mutable goods; since we acknowledge that it is of the soul alone, and voluntary, and on that account culpable? And the value of every useful discipline dealing with this matter lies in this; that rejecting and restraining the movement, we turn our wills from the transience of temporal goods to the enjoyment of the everlasting good.

3. *E.* I see; and I know the things you say are true, almost as if I touched them. For there is nothing that I perceive so surely and so intimately as that I have a will, and that I am moved by it to enjoy anything. For if the will by which I will or do not will is not mine, I find absolutely nothing that I can call mine. Wherefore, if I do anything wrong by it, to whom should it be ascribed but me? For since the good God made me, and since I can do nothing rightly except by my will, it is clear enough that it was given by the good God for that purpose. If, moreover, the movement of the will by which it is turned this way and that were not voluntary and placed in our power, a man were not to be praised when he twists, as it were, the axis of his will toward higher things, nor reproached when he twists it toward lower; and he should not be admonished at all to neglect those lower things and to will not to live wrongly, but to live rightly. But anyone who thinks that a man should not be so admonished, deserves to be banished from the company of men.

CHAPTER II

Why God's foreknowledge does not take free will away from sinners, a question that troubles very many men.

4.   This being the case, I am disturbed more than I can tell you, as to how it can be both that God foreknows all future things, and that we do not sin by necessity. For whoever says

that anything can come to pass otherwise than as God has foreknown it, is laboring with maddest impiety to do away with God's foreknowledge. Therefore God foreknew that the first man would sin; for anyone will concede this to be necessary, who agrees with me that God foreknows all things to come. This being the case, I do not say that He should not have made man, for *He* made him good, nor is the sin of him whom God himself made good anything prejudicial to God; rather indeed has He shown His goodness in making him, and shown likewise His justice in punishing him, and His mercy in forgiving him. And so I do not say that He should not have made him, but I do say this: that since He foreknew that man would sin, it was necessary that that should come to pass which God foreknew would be. How then is the will free, where necessity seems so inevitable?

5. *A.* You have knocked vigorously: may God's mercy be with us, and may He open to them that knock. Nevertheless I believe that men for the most part are tormented by that question only because they do not seek with piety, and are quicker at excusing than at confessing their sins. For there are some who like to think that there is no divine providence at the head of human affairs, and who, entrusting their bodies and their souls to the event of chance, give themselves over to lusts that rend and slay. Denying divine judgments, they evade human judgments, and think to drive away those who accuse them by the patronage of fortune, whom nevertheless they are wont to represent in their statues and paintings as blind; so that either they think themselves better than she by whom they are ruled, or acknowledge that they too perceive and say these things in a like blindness. Nor is it absurd to concede to such men that they do all things by chance (*casibus*), when they fall (*cadunt*) in the doing. But against this opinion, full of the maddest and most foolish error, enough has been said, I think, in our second discourse.

But others indeed do not venture to deny that God's providence presides over human life, but yet prefer, in impious error, to believe that it is weak, or unjust, or evil, rather than with piety to confess their sins as suppliants. If all these would let themselves be persuaded that when they think of what is best and justest and most powerful, they should believe that God's goodness and justice and power are far greater than anything their minds can conceive; considering themselves, they would then understand that they should be grateful to God, even if He had willed them to be something lower than they are, and with every bone and fiber of their conscious being would cry out: *I said, Lord, be merciful unto me: heal my soul; for I have sinned against thee.** Thus they so that not puffed up by things found, nor impatient over things not found, they would by knowledge become better prepared to see, and by ignorance more humble to seek. But to you, who, I doubt not, are already persuaded of this, I say: see how easily I shall answer you on this great question, when you shall first have answered a few questions of mine.

CHAPTER III

God's foreknowledge does not so act that we do not sin by free will.

6. It is this, to be sure, that troubles you, and that you cannot understand—why these two things are not conflicting and opposed: that God has foreknowledge of all things to come, and that we sin, not by necessity, but by our own will. For, say you, if God foreknows that a man is going to sin, it is necessary that he should sin; but if it is necessary, there is then no choice of the will in sinning, but rather an inevitable and fixed necessity. By this reasoning, forsooth, you are afraid lest it should follow either that God's foreknowledge of all things to come is impiously denied; or that, if we would be led to wisdom by the sure paths of divine mercy;

---

*Psalm XLI, 4.

cannot deny this, we admit that man sins not by choice, but by necessity. Is there anything else that troubles you?

E. Nothing else at the moment.

A. You think, then, that the whole scheme of things that God foreknows comes to pass, not by will, but by necessity?

E. Entirely so, I think.

A. Wake up then, take a look at yourself, and tell me if you can, what sort of will you are going to have tomorrow. Will it be to sin, or not to sin?

E. I do not know.

A. Do you think that God too does not know?

E. By no means would I think that.

A. If then He knows your will of tomorrow, and foresees the future wills of all men who are or who will be, much more surely does He foresee what He is going to do regarding just and impious men.

E. Assuredly, if I say that God foreknows my own works, much more confidently can I say that He foreknows His own works, and foresees with certainty what He is going to do.

A. Are you not then on your guard lest it be said to you that even God will do what He is going to do, not by will, but by necessity; if all things that He foreknows come to pass by necessity, not by will?

E. When I said that all those things come to pass by necessity which God has foreknown were to be, I was looking at those things alone which happen in His creation, but not those which are in God himself; for these do not happen, but eternally are.

A. God, then, is not occupied with His creation?

E. He has decreed once for all how the order of the would He has created is to be carried out, and does not administer anything by a new act of will.

A. Does God make no one happy?

E. Surely He does.

A. Then surely He does so when that person becomes happy.

E. True.

A. If, therefore, for example, you are going to be happy a year hence He is going to make you happy a year from now.

E. Yes.

A. Therefore He foreknows today that you are going to be made happy a year from now.

E. He has always foreknown it: I agree that He foreknows it now too, if it is going to be so.

7. *A.* Tell me, pray, are not you His creature, and will not your happiness be made in you?

E. I am indeed His creature, and in me will it come to pass that I shall be happy.

A. Therefore your happiness will come to pass in you not by will, but by necessity, God doing it.

E. His will is my necessity.

A. So, then, you will be happy against your will?

E. If I had the power to be happy I should surely be so; for even now I wish to be, and am not; because it is not I, but He that makes me happy.

A. Most excellently does the truth cry out from you. For you cannot perceive anything else to be in our power, except that which we do when we will. Wherefore nothing is so completely in our power as the will itself. For it is present with absolutely no interval, as soon as we will. And therefore we can say rightly that we grow old not by will, but by necessity; or that we die not by will, but by necessity; and anything else like that. But who but a crazy man would say that we do not will by will?

Wherefore, although God foreknows our wills to be, it does not thereby follow that we do not will a thing by our will. You said about happiness that you could not become happy through yourself, and said it as if I would deny it. But I say, when you are going to be happy you are not going to be happy against your will, but wanting to be happy. When, therefore, God foreknows your future happiness, it cannot come to pass otherwise than as He has foreknown it, else there is no foreknowledge; nevertheless we are not obliged to think what is most absurd and far removed from the truth, that you are going to be happy when you do not want to. Moreover, just as God's foreknowledge, which today is certain of your future happiness, does not take away your will for happiness when you shall have begun to be happy; so also a culpable will, if you are going to have one, will be none the less your own will because God foreknows that it is to be so.

8.   For mark, I beg you, with what blindness it is said that if God has foreknown my future will, it is necessary that I will what he has foreknown, since naught can come to pass otherwise than as He has foreknown. But if it is necessary, it must be acknowledged that I will no longer by will, but by necessity. O strange unreason! How then could it not be otherwise than as God has foreknown, if that should not be a will which He foreknew would be a will? I pass over that equally monstrous thing which a little while ago I said was said by the same man: It is necessary that I so will—thus endeavoring to take away the will and to substitute necessity. For if it is necessary that he so will, how then does he will when there is no will?

But if, speaking in another way, he says that, because it is necessary that he should will, the will itself is not in his power, he is met by what you said just now when I asked you whether you are going to be happy against your will. For you answered that you would be happy now if it were in your power; saying that you wanted to, but were not yet able. Whereupon I interjected that the truth had cried out from you. For we can deny that we have a power only when what we want is not there. But when we will, if the will itself is not there, we surely do not will. But if it cannot happen that while we will we do not will, a will is certainly present to those who will; nor is anything else in their power but what is present to those who will it. Therefore our will would not be a will if it were not in our power.

Moreover, because it is in our power it is free to us. For

that is not free to us. that we have not, or cannot have, in our power. And so it comes about both that we do not deny that God foreknows all that is to be, and that notwithstanding we may will what we will. For when He foreknows our will, it will be that very will that He foreknows. It will therefore be a will, because His foreknowledge is of a will. Nor can it be a will if it is not in our power. Therefore He is also foreknowing of the power. Therefore that power is not taken from me by His foreknowledge, but because of it will be more surely present to me; because He whose foreknowledge errs not has foreknown that it will be present to me.

E. Behold, I no longer deny that whatsoever God foreknows must needs come to pass, and that He so foreknows our sins that there yet remains to us a will that is free, and placed in our power.

CHAPTER IV

A foreknowing God does not compel men to sin, and therefore punishes sins justly.

9. *A.* What is it then that troubles you? Have you forgotten what we established in our first discussion; and will you deny that we do not sin by the compulsion of anyone—higher, or lower, or equal—but by our own will?

E. Assuredly I do not dare to deny any of these things; but I confess that I still do not see why these two things—God's foreknowledge of our sins, and our free choice in sinning—are not opposed to one another. For we must acknowledge that God is just, and also foreknowing. But I would like to know what sort of justice that is, which punishes sins that have to be committed; or how is it that they do not have to be, when He foreknows that they will be; or why anything that is necessarily done in his creation is not to be imputed to the Creator.

10. *A.* Why then do you think that our free choice is opposed to

God's foreknowledge? Is it because it is foreknowledge, or because it is God's foreknowledge?

E. Rather because it is God's.

A. Well, if you foreknew that someone was going to sin, would it not be necessary that he should sin?

E. Surely it would be necessary that he should sin, for it would not be foreknowledge, if I did not foreknow a certainty.

A. Therefore, it is necessary that what God foreknows must happen, not because it is God's foreknowledge, but simply because it is foreknowledge; for if what He foreknew were not certain, it would be no foreknowledge.

E. I agree: but why are you making these points?

A. Because if I am not mistaken you would not necessarily compel a man to sin who you foreknew was going to sin; although without doubt he will sin, for otherwise you would not foreknow that it will be so.[1] And so, just as these two are not opposed, that you know by your foreknowledge what another is going to do of his own will; so God, while compelling no one to sin, nevertheless foresees those who will sin of their own volition.

11. Why then may He not with justice punish those things, which foreknowing He does not compel? For just as you do not by your memory compel past things to have been done, in like manner God does not by His foreknowledge compel the doing of things that are to be. And just as you remember certain things that you have done, and yet do not remember all that you have done; so God foreknows all things of which He is the author, but is nevertheless not the author of all that He foreknows. But of the things of which He is not the evil author, He is the just avenger. Understand from this, therefore, that God punishes sins justly, because He does not do those things which He foreknows are to be. For if He should not visit sinners with punishment because He foreknows that

---

[1] Nor would your very foreknowledge compel him to sin though without doubt he were destined to sin, for otherwise you would not foreknow that that would be. M.

they will sin, neither should He visit well-doers with rewards, because He foresees equally that they will do right.

Rather indeed we should confess, that it is proper to His foreknowledge that nothing that is to be is hidden from Him, and [that it is proper] to His justice that sins, because they are committed by free will, are not so done unpunished by His judgment, just as they are not compelled by His foreknowledge to be done.

CHAPTER V

God is to be praised for continuing to create even creatures that sin and are a prey to unhappiness.

12.   Now as to that third question of yours—why whatever happens necessarily in the creature is not to be imputed to the Creator—that rule of piety, which it is fitting that we recall, will readily remind you that we owe an act of thanksgiving to our Creator; for His generous goodness should justly be praised, even if He had made us creatures of a lower order. For even though our soul may be wasted by sinning, it is nevertheless better and more sublime than if it should be transformed into this visible light. And you see assuredly how souls praise God for the excellence of this light, even when given over to the senses of the body. Wherefore, let not the fact that sinful souls are reproached move you to say in your heart, that it were better they had not been. For they are reproached in comparison to themselves, when one thinks what they would be if they had not chosen to sin. Nevertheless, to God their creator should be given the most excellent praise that men can give; not only because He justly orders sinners in their place, but also because He has made them such, that even soiled with sin they are in no way surpassed by the dignity of corporeal light, which yet is rightly praised.

13.   But I advise you to be careful to avoid saying that it were better if they had not been, and instead to say that they ought to have been made otherwise. For if by true reasoning you

think of anything better, know that God, as creator of all goods, has made it. But it is not true reason, but envious weakness, when you have thought of anything better to make, to want nothing else inferior to it to be made; just as if, having seen the heavens, you should be unwilling to have the earth made—quite unjustly. For you would rightly find fault if you saw the earth made and the heavens left out, since you would say that it should be made in such manner as you can conceive the heavens to be. When, therefore, you saw that made to whose appearance you were wanting to transform the earth, but called not this earth, but the heavens; I think that not being cheated of the better thing because an inferior thing too was made, and was the earth, you should nowise cavil. Again, in the earth, so great is the variety among its parts, that nothing that pertains to the form of the earth can be thought of that God the creator of all things has not somewhere made in the whole mass of it. For from the most fruitful and pleasant land to the most treacherous and sterile, you may so pass by intermediate degrees, that you would not venture to find fault with any land, except in comparison with a better; and would so ascend through all degrees of praise that when you find the highest type of land you would yet be unwilling to have it the only kind.

But now how great the distance between the whole earth and the heavens. For there lies between them a watery and an airy nature; and compounded of these four elements a variety of other forms and species, to us innumerable, but numbered by God. There can, therefore, be things in nature which you cannot conceive by your reason. But it cannot be that what you conceive by true reason does not exist; nor can you think of anything better in creation that has escaped the artificer of creation. For the human mind is connected by its nature with the divine reason on which it depends; so that when it says, "This should be made better than that," if it speaks truly, and sees that it speaks truly, it sees this in those reasons with which it is connected. One should therefore believe that God has made what by true reason he knows should have been made by Him, even if he does not see it in actual things. Because even if he were unable to see the heavens with his eyes, and notwithstanding concluded by true reason that they should have been made, he should believe that they have been made, although he does not see them with his eyes. For he would not have been able to see by his thinking that they should have been made, except in those reasons by which all things are made. But what is not in those reasons, to the same degree no one can see by true thinking as it is not true.

14. In this matter most men go wrong when they have seen the better things with their minds, they look for them with their eyes in inappropriate places; as if someone understanding perfect roundness by his reason should be vexed because he does not find such a thing in a nut, never having seen any round bodies except fruits of this sort. For so some men, when by truest reason they see that that creature is better, which, although it has free will, has its will ever fixed on God and never sins, grieve when they regard the sins of men, not that they do not cease from sinning, but that they were made, saying, "He should have so made us that we would ever enjoy his immutable truth, and never want to sin." Let them not complain, let them not be angry; because by making those to whom He gave whichever power they wished He did not thereby compel these to sin. And such are certain angels, who have never sinned, nor will ever sin. Wherefore, if that creature pleases you, that by a most persevering will does not sin, there is no doubt that you would by right reason place him higher than a sinner; but just as you place him higher in your thoughts, so God has placed him higher by His ordinance. Believe, then, that there is such a creature in the thrones above, and in the sublimity of the heavens: because if the Creator showed His goodness by creating him whose future sins He foresaw, He would by no means not show that

goodness by making a creature that He foreknew would not sin.

15.   For that sublime creature has eternal happiness, enjoying its Creator forever, which it merits by its unalterable will to hold to justice. Next, that sinful nature too has its own rank, having lost its happiness to sins, but not having forfeited its power of regaining it. Such a one is indeed higher than that nature that forever wills to sin, being as it were a mean between it and that other which is fixed in its will for justice, and regaining its height by humility of repentance. For even from that creature which God foreknew would not only sin, but even continue in the will to sin, He did not withhold the bounty of His goodness by not creating it. For just as a straying horse is better than a stone, which does not go astray because it has no sense or movement of its own; so is that creature more excellent which sins by free will, than that which sins not because it has no free will. And just as I would praise wine good in its kind, and censure a man drunken with this wine, and notwithstanding place this same man, just censured and still drunken, above the praised wine by which he was made drunken; so is a corporeal creature rightly to be praised in its degree, while they are to be censured who by its intemperate use are turned away from the perception of truth; although again these same men, now perverted and as it were reeling, are to be preferred to that same creature, laudable in its own order, for greed of which they have been undone; not indeed in the fault of their vices, but yet in the dignity of their nature.

16.   Every soul is better than every body, and no sinful soul, however far it may have fallen, becomes a body or by any transformation, ever ceases to be a soul; and so it never loses its superiority to a body. Among bodies, moreover, light is preeminent. It follows therefore that the last soul is to be placed ahead of the first body. It may happen that the body

of one soul is to be placed ahead of the body of another soul, but ahead of the soul itself, never.

Why then should we not praise God, and praise with praise ineffable Him who, when He made those souls which would ever continue in the laws of justice, made also other souls, which He foresaw would sin, or even continue in sin; since even such are better than those which cannot sin because they have no rational and free judgment of will? And yet these in their turn are better than the most dazzling light of any bodies whatsoever: a light which some worship, albeit in great error, as the substance of the supreme God himself. Therefore if in the order of corporeal creatures the beauty of good things is graduated so continuously from the stars in their orbits to the number of our hairs,[1] that it is foolish to ask, "What is this?" "Of what use is that?", for all things are created in their own order: how much more foolish, then, to say this of any soul whatsoever, which, however much it is degraded and shorn of its beauty, beyond question will always surpass the dignity of all bodies.

17.   For reason values things in one way, and use in another. Reason values by the light of truth, so that by right judgment it may subordinate lesser things to greater; but use generally leans towards habit and convenience, and thus values those things more which truth proves to be less. For while reason places celestial bodies far above terrestrial, who among carnal men would not rather that many stars should fail in the sky, than that one plant should fail in his field, or one cow in his herd? But just as men make naught of the judgment of little children, or at any rate wait tolerantly for it to be corrected, when these, leaving out a few in whose love they delight, would rather have any one of other men die than their pet bird—particularly if the man were someone who frightened them, and the bird a sweet singer, and beautiful: so those

---

[1] But if in the order of corporeal creatures, from the very choruses of the stars even to the number of our hairs, so by degrees is the beauty of good things interwoven, etc. M.

who by maturity of soul have progressed toward wisdom find men who value things ignorantly, and who praise God in the lesser things of creation, because such things are better suited to their carnal senses; but who in the higher and better things praise Him not, or praise Him less; or who even censure and try to improve on Him; or who do not believe He is the creator of them. But the wiser, if they cannot correct such judgments, are wont to make naught of them; or until such time as they may be able to correct them to tolerate and endure them with an equal mind.

CHAPTER VI

No one says truly that he would rather not be than be unhappy.

18.   These things being so, they are far from the truth who think that the sins of the creature are to be imputed to the Creator; notwithstanding that those things will necessarily come to pass that He has foreknown were to be. So when you say you cannot see why anything that happens necessarily in His creature is not to be imputed to Him, I, on the contrary, can find no way, and assert moreover that no way can be found, and that there is absolutely no way, in which anything can be imputed to God which, though it happens necessarily in His creation, is yet done by the will of sinners.

For if someone should say: I would rather not be, than be as unhappy as I am; I should answer: That is not true. For even now, unhappy, you are; and it is only because you wish to be that you do not want to die; and so, when you do not want to be unhappy, you want nevertheless to be. Give thanks, therefore, that you are wanting something, so that your unwillingness may be removed. For wanting you are, even though it is only wanting not to be unhappy. But if you are ungrateful for your wanting to be, you are rightly compelled to be that which you do not want. Because, therefore, even though you are ungrateful, you have what you want, I praise

the goodness of God; but because you, ungrateful, suffer
what you would not, I praise the justice of Him who orders
all things.

19.   If he should say: It is not because I would rather be unhappy than not be at all, that I am unwilling to die, but for
fear that after death I may be still more unhappy. I answer:
If this is unjust, it will not be so with you; but if it is just,
let us praise Him by whose laws it will be so. If he should
say: Why may I presume that if it is unjust it will not be so?
I will answer: Because if you were in your own power, either
you would not be unhappy, or you would justly be unhappy
because you were ruling yourself unjustly; or if you wished
to rule yourself justly and were unable, you would not be in
your own power, but either in the power of no one, or of
someone else. If you were in the power of no one, you would
be either willing or unwilling. But you cannot be unwilling
unless overpowered by some force; but again, no force can
overcome you which is in no one's power. But if, willing, you
are in the power of no one, this amounts to saying that you
are in your own power; and so, either you are justly unhappy
because you are ruling yourself unjustly, or you should yet
give thanks to your Creator that you can want what you will.
But if you are not in your own power, he in whose power
you are will be either a stronger, or a weaker. But if he is
weaker, the fault is yours, and your unhappiness is just;
because if you will you can overcome a weaker. But if a
stronger has you, the weaker, in his power, you can in no way
think that an arrangement so right is unjust. Most truly,
therefore, was it said: If this is unjust, it will not be so; but
if it is just, let us praise Him by whose laws it will be so.

CHAPTER VII

Being is loved even by the unhappy, because they are from Him who supremely is.

20.   If he should say: It is because I now exist that I would rather be unhappy than not be at all; but if, before I was, I could have been consulted, I would have chosen not to exist, rather than be unhappy. But now it is a part of that same unhappiness, by which I do not want what I should want, that though unhappy I am afraid not to exist; for I ought to want not to exist, rather than be unhappy. I now admit that I would rather be unhappy than be nothing; but I am the more foolish to want it, the more unhappy I am; and am moreover the more unhappy, the more truly I see that I ought not to want it. I shall answer: Take care, rather, that you do not err in thinking you see the truth. For if you were happy, you would certainly rather exist than not exist; and even now, while you are unhappy, you prefer to be rather than not be at all, although you do not want to be unhappy. Consider, therefore, with all your powers, how great a good is existence itself, which both the happy and the unhappy want. For if you weigh the matter well you will see that you are unhappy in the measure that you do not draw near to that which supremely is. For you will see that in the measure you think it better that one should not exist, rather than be unhappy, so far do you fail to see that which supremely is; and for this reason you yet want to exist, because you are from Him who supremely is.

21.   And so, if you would flee unhappiness, love in yourself this very thing, namely, that you exist. For if you want more and more to be, you will draw near to that which supremely is; so give thanks that you now are. For although you may be inferior to those who are happy, you are yet superior to those things which have not the will for happiness, many of which are yet praised by unhappy men.

All things, nevertheless, are rightly to be praised for the very fact that they are; because by the fact that they are, they are good. For the more you love being, the more you will long for the life eternal, and will yearn to be so formed that your affections will not be temporal, branded and marked by the love of temporal things. For these temporal things are not, until they come to be; and even while they are, they are passing; and when they shall have passed, they will not be: and so, when they are going to be, they are not yet; but when they have passed, they are no more. How then will these things be held enduringly, when the beginning of their being is but a progress toward their being not. But he who loves being approves these things in so far as they are, and loves that which eternally is. And if his love of those was making him inconstant, he will be made strong by his love of that eternal being; and if he was being dispersed by his love of transient things, he will be made firm and whole by his love for that which endures, and will stand erect and affirm his own being, as he would fain have done when he feared not to be, and could not stand because entangled in his love of things that pass.

Be not cast down, therefore, but rather greatly lifted up, because you would rather be, even if unhappy, than not be unhappy because you are nothing. For if to this beginning of wanting to be you add more being and yet more, you will rise and be built up into that which supremely is; and so you will keep yourself from all taint by which that which is lowest passes so that it is not [ceases to be], and with itself brings down the strength of its lover. Thus it will happen that he who would rather not be, lest he be unhappy, since he is unable not to be, must be unhappy. But he who loves his being more than he hates to be unhappy, by adding to that which he loves shuts out that which he hates; for when he shall have begun perfectly to be in his own kind, he will not be unhappy.

CHAPTER VIII

Non-being is chosen by no one, not even by those who kill themselves.

22.   For see how foolish and inconsistent it is to say: I would rather not be, than be unhappy. For he who says: I would rather this than that, chooses something. But not to be is not something, but nothing; and therefore you can in no way rightly choose, when what you choose does not exist. You say that you wish indeed to be, although you are unhappy, but that you ought not to have wished it. What, then, ought you to wish? Not to be, rather, you say. If you ought to wish this, then it is better. But what does not exist cannot be better. Therefore you ought not to wish it; and the instinct by which you do not wish it is truer than the opinion by which you think that you ought to wish it. Then again, if anyone chooses rightly something to be sought, he is necessarily made better by attaining it. But he cannot be made better who will not exist: no one therefore can rightly choose not to be. Nor ought we to be disturbed by the judgment of those who are driven by their misery to destroy themselves. For either they are fleeing to where they think they will be better off, which is not contrary to our reasoning however they may have thought; or, if they think they are not going to exist at all, much less should the false choice of those who choose nothing disturb us. For how will I follow him who, if I ask what he chooses, answers: Nothing? For he who chooses not to be is proved to choose nothing, even if he be unwilling so to answer.

23.   Let me say, however, if I can, what I think on this whole matter. I think that no one who kills himself, or who desires in any way to die, has any instinctive feeling that he is not going to exist after death, although he may to some extent hold this in his opinion. For opinion is a matter of true or erroneous reasoning or belief; but the force of instinctive

feeling is from habit and nature.[1] But that a thing may be one in opinion, and another in feeling, is easily seen from the fact that we frequently believe that we should do one thing, and like to do another. And sometimes feeling is more truthful than opinion, if the opinion is from error and the feeling from nature; as when a sick man is frequently delighted and benefited by cold water, which he nevertheless believes will hurt him if he drinks it. Sometimes opinion is more truthful than instinct; as when he believes medical science, that cold water is bad for him, when it will be bad for him, and he none the less likes to drink it. Sometimes both are true; as when what is good for him, he not only so believes, but likes. Sometimes both are in error; as when what is bad for him he both believes is good and does not cease to like. But a right opinion is often wont to correct a wrong habit; or, again, a wrong opinion may corrupt a right nature, so great is the power of reason in its rule and sway. When, therefore, anyone believing that he will not exist after death is yet driven by unbearable troubles to an utter longing for death, and decides for death and lays hold on it, he has in opinion the erroneous idea of vanishing utterly, but in instinct the natural desire for rest. But what is at rest is not nothing; rather indeed is it more than what is unquiet. For unrest changes conditions, so that one thing destroys another; but rest has constancy, which is what is chiefly understood when we say that a thing *is*. And so all that seeking in the will to die is directed, not so that he who dies may not exist, but that he may rest. So while he mistakenly believes that he will no longer be, he none the less by nature longs to be at rest; that is, to be yet more. Wherefore, as it can in no way happen that anyone should desire not to exist, it ought never to happen that anyone is ungrateful to that goodness of the Creator for that which he is.

---

[1] For opinion is either in the error or in the truth of the thinker or the believer; but feeling prevails by habit or nature. M.

CHAPTER IX

The wretchedness of the souls of sinners contributes to the perfection of the universe.

24.　　If he says: It would not have been difficult or troublesome for almighty God so to make all things that each should have its own order, and so that no creature would be unhappy. For being almighty He would not lack the power, and being good He would not grudge it. I answer: The order of creatures so descends by just degrees from the highest to the lowest, that he is the one who grudges who says, This should not have been; and he who says, This should have been so and so, grudges also. For if he wishes it to be something higher, that exists already, and in such measure that it should not be added to, for it is perfect. He therefore who says, This should be so and so, either wishes to add to a higher that is perfect, and thus will be intemperate and unjust; or he wishes to do away with it, and will be wicked and ill-willed. But he who says: This should not exist, will be no less wicked and ill-willed, since he is not willing that it should be, while he is yet constrained to praise that which is inferior to it. It is as if he should say there should be no moon; while he must either acknowledge, or foolishly and contentiously deny, that even the light of a lamp, though far inferior in brightness, is yet beautiful in its own kind in the darkness of earth, and seemly and meet for the uses of night, and in all these uses thoroughly praiseworthy in its small way. How therefore will he rightly venture to say: There should be no moon in the universe; when he know that if he said: There should be no lamp, he would be laughed at. But if he does not say there should be no moon, but seeing the sun says that the moon should be like it; he does not realize that what he is saying is: There should be no moon, but there should be two suns. Wherein he errs doubly: desiring to add to the perfection of things by wanting another sun, and desiring to diminish it by taking away the moon.

25.   But perhaps he may say that he does not complain of the moon's inferior brightness, so that the moon is not unhappy; but he laments for souls, not that they are obscure, but because they are unhappy. Let him make all he can of the fact that the brightness of the moon is not unhappy, just as the brightness of the sun is not happy. For although they are celestial bodies, they are, after all, bodies, so far as concerns the light which can be perceived by bodily eyes. But no bodies, considered as bodies, can be either happy or unhappy, although they may be the bodies of happy or unhappy men. But the differences of souls are none the less analogous to those of the lights. For in contemplating the differences of bodies, and seeing that some are brighter, you would be unjust if you should seek to take away those that you see to be darker, or to make them equal to the brighter; for referring all things to the perfection of the universe, you see that in the measure that they are more or less bright among themselves, they have all of them being; nor would the world seem perfect to you unless, where greater things were, the lesser were not lacking. In like manner you may think of the differences of souls, in which you will find correspondingly that you may know that the unhappiness which you lament is strong to serve this purpose, also in order that those souls may not be lacking to the perfection of the universe, which ought to have become unhappy because they have willed to be sinful. And so far from true is it that God should not have made such, that He is praised for making even creatures far inferior to unhappy souls.

26.   But another objection which he may advance is still less reasonable. For he says: If even our unhappiness completes the perfection of the universe, something would be lacking to this perfection if we were always happy. Wherefore, if the soul does not come to unhappiness except by sinning, our sins too are necessary to the perfection of the world that God has made. How then does He justly punish sins, without which His creation would not be full and perfect?

The reply to this is that not the sins themselves, or the unhappiness itself, are necessary to the perfection of the world, but that souls as souls, which, if they will, sin, and sinning are made unhappy. For if, their sins being taken away, the unhappiness persists, or even if it precedes the sins, the order and government of the universe are rightly said to be deformed. Again, if sins are committed and there is no unhappiness, right order is equally disgraced. But when happiness is the lot of those who sin not, the world is perfect; and it is no less perfect when unhappiness is the lot of sinners. But because those souls are not lacking which become unhappy when they sin and happy when they do right, the world is always full and perfect with all natures. For sin and the punishment of sin are not properly natures, but conditions of nature: the former being voluntary, the latter is applied in expiation, so that the nature is ordered where it may not be a disgrace, and made to conform to the glory of the universe,[1] so that the penalty of sin corrects the disgrace of sin.

27.   Hence it comes about that a superior creature who sins is punished by inferior creatures, because these are so low that they can be honored even by base souls, and so conform to the honor of the universe. For what is so great in a house as a man; and what so low and mean as the sewer of a house? And yet a slave caught in some offense for which, as punishment, he has to clean the sewer, honors that even by his disgrace; and both of these things—the slave's disgrace and the cleaning of the sewer—now joined and reduced to a unity certain of its own kind, are so fitted and woven into the household order that it harmonizes by its beauty with a perfectly ordered world.[2] Yet if this slave had not willed to offend, other provision for clearning the household necessaries would not have been wanting in the domestic management.

---

[1] The former is applied as voluntary, the latter as penal, in order that it may set the soul straight, where it may not be base for it to be such, and may force it to agree with the glory of the universe. M.

[2] That it befits its universality by a most excellently ordered beauty. M.

And what is so low among things as every earthly body? And yet even a sinful soul so beautifies this corruptible flesh, as to provide it with the most seemly aspect, and with living movement. Such a soul is therefore not fitted for a heavenly home on account of sin, but is fitted to an earthly through punishment; so that whatever it may have chosen, the fair world of which God is creator and ruler may be ordered in most seemly parts. For when the best souls dwell in the lowest creatures, they do not beautify them by their unhappiness, which they have not, but by right use of them. But if sinful souls were allowed to dwell in the highest places, that would be unseemly, because they do not harmonize with those things that they can neither use rightly nor confer any honor upon.

28.   Therefore, although this terrestrial sphere is numbered among things corruptible; yet keeping as best it can the image of higher things, it does not cease to show us examples and signs of these. For if we see some good and great man burned up, so far as his body is concerned, at the call of duty and honor, we do not call this a punishment for his sins, but a proof of his fortitude and patience, and we love him more when foulest corruption has devoured his members than if he had not suffered in this fashion, and marvel indeed that the nature of the soul has not changed with the mutability of the body. But when we see the members of a hardened criminal consumed by such a punishment, we approve the order of the law. Both of these tortures therefore complete the world; the first, however, by desert of virtue, the second of sin. But if after those fires, or even before, we should see that noble man changed so as to prepare him for a heavenly abode, and raised up to the stars, we would surely rejoice. But if we should see the depraved criminal, whether before or after punishment, with his same wickedness of will raised to an everlasting seat of honor in heaven, who would not be offended? So it happens that both men may give honor to inferior creatures, but only one to higher creatures. We are reminded

from this to note both that the first man so adorned the mortality of this flesh that punishment might fit the sin, and that our Lord so adorned it that mercy might free from sin. For though a just man, continuing in justice, could have a mortal body, not so could the wicked man, while he is wicked, attain to the immortality of the saints, that is, sublime and angelic immortality—not the immortality of those angels of whom the Apostle says: *Know ye not that we shall judge angels?** but of those of whom our Lord says: *And they will be equal to the Angels of God.*† For those who desire equality to the angels for their own vain glory do not thereby want to be equal to the angels, but that the angels should be equal to them; and so, persisting in such a wish, they will be made equal in punishment to the rebellious angels, who love their own power better than the power of almighty God. For to such, placed on the left hand because they sought not God by the gate of humility which our Lord Jesus Christ shows in himself, but have lived in pride and hardness of heart, will be said: *Depart into everlasting fire, which is prepared for the devil and his angels.*‡

CHAPTER X

By what right the devil has possessed man, and by what right God has freed him.

29. For while there are two sources of sin, one from a man's umprompted thinking, the other by persuasion of someone else — to which I think the Prophet refers when he says: *Cleanse thou me of secret sins, and from the sins of others spare thy servant§*—both are indeed voluntary; for just as one does not sin unwillingly by his own thinking, so when he yields to the evil persuasions of another, he surely does not

*I Cor. VI, 3.
†Luke, XX, 36.
‡Matt. XXV, 41.
§Psalm XIX, 12, 13.

yield except of his own will. But it is nevertheless a more grievous fault, not only to sin of one's own accord without any persuasion, but also by malice and deceit to persuade others to sin, than to be led to sin by the persuasion of another. Therefore justice is preserved by God in punishing both of these sins. For this too was weighed in the balance of equity, that man was not denied to the power of the devil, who had made man subject to him by his evil persuasion; for it were unfair that the devil should not have mastery over him whom he had taken; as it could nowise happen that the perfect justice of the true and supreme God [which extends to each and every thing] should fail to give order even to the downfall of sinners. And yet, because man had sinned less than the devil, that very fact availed him for regaining his salvation, that he was in bondage to the prince of this world, that is of that lowest and mortal part of things; and hence to the prince of sinners and lord of death so far as mortal flesh is concerned. For so man is fearful in his consciousness of his mortality, and in dread of harm and destruction from the meanest and feeblest, and even the tiniest of living creatures; and unsure of things to come, and unable to control unlawful delights, particularly pride, by persuasion of which he fell, and by which vice alone the medicine of mercy is rejected, he is wont to break down. For who has such need of mercy as a wretched man? And who is so unworthy of mercy as the proud wretch?

30.   From this it came about that that Word of God, *by whom all things were made,** and in whom all angelic blessedness has its joy, held out His mercy to our wretchedness, and *the Word was made flesh, and dwelt among us.*† For thus man, not equal to the angels, could eat of the Bread of Angels, if the Bread of Angels itself deigned to become equal to men. For He did not so descend to us as to forsake them; but was at the same time whole to them and whole to us, feeding

*John, I, 3.
†*Ibid*. I, 14.

them inwardly by His Godhead, teaching us outwardly by
the manhood that we too have, and through faith making
those fit to feed equally by the sight. For the rational
creature is fed by that Word as by food most excellent. The
human soul moreover is rational, though held in mortal
bonds as a penalty for sin, and so reduced in dignity that it
must endeavor to understand invisible things by conjecture
from visible things. Therefore the food of the rational
creature is made visible, not by change of its nature, but of
our condition, so that we pursuing visible things may be
called back to it, invisible. Thus the soul finds Him Whom it
had forsaken in its inward pride outwardly humble, and by
imitation of His humility will return to the invisible height.

31.   And the Word of God, the only Son of God, clothed as a
man, made the devil, whom He has ever had and ever will
have subject to His laws, subject to man also; not wresting
aught from him by violent mastery, but overcoming him by
the law of justice. For the devil, having deceived the woman,
and through her brought about the downfall of the man, was
laying claim to all the descendants of the first man as sinners
by the law of death; in a wicked desire to do harm, indeed,
but none the less by a most equitable right. This power of
his held good until he put to death the Just One, in whom he
could show nothing deserving of death; not only because He
was slain for no offence, but also because He was born without that lust, to which the devil had subjected those whom he
had taken, so that whatever was born of it he would retain as
if it were fruit of his tree; by a wicked desire to possess it
indeed, but yet with a right that was not unfair. And so he
is most justly compelled to let go those who believe in Him
whom he put to death unjustly; so that dying in this world
they cancel the debt, and living eternally they live in Him
who paid for them what He did not owe. But those whom
the devil has persuaded to continue in unbelief he justly has
with him to share his everlasting damnation. Thus it came
about that man, whom the devil had not taken by force, but

by persuasion, was likewise not wrested from him by force; and he who was justly brought lower to serve him to whom he had consented for evil, was justly set free by Him to whom he had consented for good; because he had sinned less in consenting than had the devil in evilly persuading him.

CHAPTER XI

The creature, whether it is going to continue in justice, or to fall from it, contributes to the adornment of the universe.

32. Therefore God made all natures; not only those that would continue in virtue and justice, but also those that would sin— not in order that they might sin, but so that they might adorn the universe, whether they should will to sin or not. For if among created things those souls were lacking which so uphold the very summit of order in creation, that if they should have willed to sin the universe would be weakened and made to totter, something great would have been lacking in creation; for that would be lacking whose removal would upset the harmony and stability of things. Such are the most holy and sublime creatures of celestial or supercelestial powers, whom God alone rules, and to whom moreover the whole world is subject. Without the just and perfect offices of these the universe could not be. Again, if there were wanting those natures which might either sin or not sin; though the order of the universe would not be less, even so much would be lacking. For they are rational souls, unequal indeed in office to those higher ones, but equal in nature; and there are yet many grades of things created by the supreme God, inferior to these, and yet worthy of praise.

33. Therefore the nature of that sublimer office is such that not only if it did not exist, but even if it should sin, the order of the universe would be diminished. That of the lower office is such that only if it did not exist, but not if it sinned, the universe would be something less. To the former nature is given authority to maintain all things by its own offices, which

could not be lacking to the order of things; nor does it continue in good will because it has been given this duty, but has been given the duty because He who gave it forsaw that it would continue. And yet it does not maintain all things by its own majesty, but by cleaving to the majesty and loyally obeying the commands of Him *from whom and by whom and in whom all things are made.** But to the latter, when it does not sin, is given indeed that most high office of maintaining all things, but not as its own however, but in company with the former nature, as if to a nature which was foreknown to be peccable. For spiritual natures are in fact added together without increase or parted without diminution; so that the angelic nature was not aided in the ease of its action when the other was joined to it, nor was its action made more difficult if the other forsook its office by sinning. For spirit natures can be joined and sundered by their equality or inequality of condition, and not by location or bulk of bodies, although they may each possess individual bodies.

34.   But the soul assigned after its sin to an inferior and mortal body rules its own body not entirely according to its choice, but only as the laws of the universe permit. Such a soul is not however on that account inferior to a celestial body, to which terrestrial bodies are also subject. For the ragged garment of a condemned slave is indeed far inferior to the clothing of one well-deserving and established in the good graces of his master; but the slave himself is better than the most costly rainment, because he is a man.

The angelic nature, therefore, clings to God, in a celestial body with angelic power, and also adorns and rules an earthly body at the command of Him whose will is perceived in ways utterable. But the other, weighed down by a mortal frame, manages from within with difficult even the very body which wraps it, while on other bodies, adjacent and external to it, it acts from without with far feebler effect as best it can.

---

*Romans, XI, 36.

CHAPTER XII

The government of the universe would not be thrown into confusion even if every angelic creature should sin.

35.   Whence we conclude that these lowest of corporeal creatures would not have lacked their perfect embellishment even if those souls had not chosen to sin. For what can rule the whole rules also the part; but it does not thereby follow that what has less power can also rule the greater. For a perfect physician is also competent to cure the itch; but it does not therefore follow that one who can give advice on the itch can heal all bodily ills. And if we examine the sure reasoning by which it is proved that there should have been a creature who never had and never will sin, that same reasoning tells us that that nature refrains from sin by free will, not compelled thereto, but of its own accord. But even if it should sin (though in fact it has not sinned, just as God foreknew it would not)—nevertheless if even that should sin, the indescribable might of God's power would suffice to rule the universe; so that giving to all things what is most meet and worthy He would permit nothing base or unseemly in His whole domain. Because, whether through no powers established for this special purpose, if every angelic nature had by sinning departed from His ordinances, He would rule all things most excellently and becomingly by His own majesty. Nor would He thereby grudge being to spiritual creatures; for He has even created the corporeal nature far inferior to spiritual natures—even to sinful ones—and in such lavish goodness that there is no one who with his reason looks upon sky and earth, and upon all visible natures governed and formed and ordered in their kinds, who can either believe that they have an artificer other than God, or who does not confess that He is to be praised with praise unutterable. Or if there is no better ordering of things than that the angelic power by the goodness of its will and the excellence of its nature should oversee the disposition of the universe, even if

all the Angels had sinned they would cause no helplessness to the Creator of Angels in ruling His universe. For His goodness would not fail as if from weariness, nor His omnipotence because of any difficulty, to create others to place on the thrones which those had foresaken by sinning; nor could the spiritual creature, of whatever number, if it were condemned according to its deserts, cripple the ordinance which rightly and properly removes those to be condemned. Turn where we will, therefore, we find that we should praise beyond the power of all expression God the most excellent Creator of all natures, and most just ruler.

36.   We may leave the contemplation of the beauty of things to those who by divine gift can see it, and not attempt by words to lead those who cannot to a vision of the ineffable. But because of talkative or weak or deceitful men let us neverthless conclude with a short summary of the whole question.

CHAPTER XIII

The goodness of the creature itself is shown by its corruption, and by the blaming of its fault.

Every nature which can become less good, is good; and every nature becomes less good by corruption. For either corruption does not hurt it, and it is not corrupted; or if it is corrupted, corruption hurts it, and if it hurts it, takes away something from its good and makes it less good. For if it deprives it utterly of all good, whatever shall remain of it can no longer be corrupted; because no good will be left for corruption to hurt by taking it away. But that which corruption cannot hurt is not corrupted; and a nature which is not corrupted is incorruptible. We would therefore have a nature made incorruptible by corruption, which is a most absurd thing to say. Therefore we can say that every nature, in so far as it is a nature, is good; because if it is incorruptible, it is better than a corruptible nature; but if it is corruptible, since it becomes less good by corruption, it is without doubt good. But every nature is either corruptible or incorruptible. Therefore every nature is good. I call that a nature which is also often called a substance. Every substance, therefore, is either God, or from God; because every good is either God, or from God.

37.   These things being established and made sure as a starting point for our reasoning, give attention to what I shall say. Every rational nature, created with free judgment of will, if it continues in the enjoyment of the supreme and immutable good, is without doubt to be praised; and every nature which tends to continue is also to be praised. But every nature that does not continue in it, and does not will so to act that it may continue in it, in the measure that it is not in this state and does not act so as to be in this state, is to be blamed. If therefore a rational created nature is praised, no one doubts that He is to be praised who made it; and if it is to be blamed, no one doubts that its Creator is praised by that very blaming of it. For when we blame it because it does not will to enjoy the supreme and immutable good, that is, its Creator, we most assuredly praise Him. How great, therefore, is this good, and how beyond utterance in any tongue, and beyond all our conceiving should God the Creator of all things be praised and glorified; for without praising Him we can neither be praised nor blamed. For we cannot be blamed for not remaining in Him, unless to remain in Him were our great and chief and first good: but how can this be except that He is unutterably good? What then can be found in our sins for which to blame Him, when the blaming of our sins is no blaming unless He is praised?

38.   But even in those very things that are blamed, nothing is blamed except the fault. But the fault of anything is not blamed without praising the nature of the thing. For that which you blame is either according to nature, and is not a fault, and you are to be corrected so that you may know rightly what to blame, rather than that which you do not

rightly blame; or, if it is a fault, it must be contrary to the nature if it is rightly to be blamed. For every fault, by the very fact that it is a fault, is contrary to the nature. For if it does not harm the nature it is not a fault; but if it is a fault because it does harm the nature, it is a fault because it is opposed to the nature. But if a nature is corrupted not by its own fault, but by the fault of another nature, it is blamed unjustly, and we must ask whether that nature whose fault corrupts another nature is not corrupted by its own fault. But what else is having a fault but being corrupted by that fault? Moreover the nature which is not damaged has no fault; but that by whose fault another nature is corrupted has assuredly a fault. That nature, by whose fault another nature can be corrupted, must therefore itself first be faulty, and first corrupted by its own fault.[1] From which we conclude that every fault is contrary to nature, even to the nature of the thing of which it is a fault. Wherefore, since in any thing only the fault is blamed, and since moreover it is a fault because it is contrary to the nature of the thing whose fault it is, we cannot rightly blame the fault of anything without praising its nature. For a fault cannot rightly displease you, unless you are pleased by that which the fault impairs.

CHAPTER XIV

Not all corruption is deserving of blame.

39.   We must now see whether a nature can rightly be said to be corrupted by the fault of another, without any added fault of its own. For if a nature comes with its fault to another nature to corrupt it, and finds in it nothing corruptible, it does not corrupt it; but if it does find it, it works its corruption by the addition of its own fault. But if a stronger nature does not want to be corrupted by a weaker, it is not corrupted; but if it consents, it begins to be corrupted by its own fault

---

[1] First therefore is that nature faulty, and first is it corrupted by its own fault, by whose fault another nature also is corrupted. M.

before it is by the fault of that other. In the same way a nature cannot be corrupted by an equal nature, if it is unwilling. For whatsoever nature with a fault comes to that which is without fault to corrupt it, for that very reason does not come as an equal, but is weaker because of its fault. But if a stronger nature corrupts a weaker, it is either the fault of both, if both are depraved by wrong desire, or it is the fault of the stronger, if its nature is so preeminent that even corrupt it is superior to the weaker nature which it corrupts. For who would rightly blame the fruits of the earth because men may use them wrongly, and corrupted by their own faults corrupt these by intemperate misuse of them; while yet a man would be insane who doubted that the nature of man, even when corrupt, was more excellent and powerful than any unblemished fruits whatsoever?

40.   It can also happen that a stronger nature may corrupt one inferior to it, and this by the fault of neither; that is, if by a fault we mean something deserving of blame. For who would blame either a worthy man who sought nothing from fruits but to supply the needs of his nature, or the fruits themselves because they are destroyed by their use as food? But such is not usually called corruption, because the word is generally used to denote a fault. This too may be easily seen in things, because a more powerful nature generally, in filling its needs, corrupts an inferior one and makes it worthless; or it can be seen in the order of justice when it avenges an offence, as is exemplified in what the Apostle said: *If any man corrupt the temple of God, him will God corrupt.** Or it may be seen in the order in which mutable things give place to one another in accordance with the fitting laws given to the universe for the powers of each part. Thus if the sun should injure by its brightness the eyes of someone that were too weak to bear its light, the sun is not to be thought of as thereby satisfying

---

*I Cor. III, 17. *Si quis templum Dei corruperit, corrumpet illum Deus.* The Vulgate has *violaverit* and *disperdet* instead of *corruperit* and *corrumpet*.

any need of its nature, or as doing this by any fault; nor are even the eyes themselves to be blamed because they yielded to their owner and were opened against that light, and thus made useless for that very light. Of all corruptions, therefore, that alone which is faulty is rightly blamed; but the others either should not be called corruptions at all, or at least, since they are not faulty, cannot be deserving of blame. For blame itself, (vituperatio), because it is incurred fittingly and deservedly only by fault, is also called fault-finding.[1]

41.   But a fault, as I had started to say, is evil only because it is opposed to the nature of that thing of which it is a fault. Whence it is clear that this same thing whose fault is blamed is by nature praiseworthy; so we must altogether admit that this very blaming of faults is a praising of natures; of those natures, that is, whose faults are blamed. For because fault is opposed to nature, the more we increase the wrongness of the fault, the more we diminish the integrity of the nature.[2] When, therefore, you blame a fault, you are assuredly praising that thing whose integrity you desire; but what except a nature can have integrity? For a perfect nature is not only deserving of no blame, but even of praise according to its kind. That which you see to be wanting to the perfection of a nature you therefore call a fault; thereby showing pretty clearly that that pleases you, which by blaming its imperfection you would have perfect.

CHAPTER XV

A defect of a creature is by no means always culpable.

42.   If therefore the blaming of faults themselves only sets off the beauty and worth of the natures of which they are faults, how much more is God the creator of all natures to be

---

[1] Because it has been prepared for fault (vitium) alone, that is, is meet and due to it, is believed to have been derived from it so as to be the term for fault finding. M.

[2] For because fault is opposed to nature, so much is added to the evil nature of faults as is taken from the integrity of natures. M.

praised even in their faults, since they both have their being as natures from Him, and are faulty only in so far as they depart from His design, according to which they were made, and are rightly censured only to the extent that their censurer sees the design by which they were made, and censures in them what he does not see there. And if the design itself by which all things are made, that is, the supreme and immutable wisdom of God, is truly and supremely that which is, you see whither tends whatsoever departs from it. This defect, never-the less, would not be so deserving of blame unless it were voluntary.

For consider, if you please, whether you would rightly blame a thing for being just as it ought (owes) to be. I think not; but you would surely blame what is not as it ought to be. But no one owes what he has never received. And if anyone is in debt, to whom is he in debt but to him from whom he received to owe it? And whatever is returned in settlement of a debt is returned to him who had made the loan. And what is returned to the lawful successors of creditors is certainly returned to the very ones that succeed to it by right. Else would it not be a return, but a cession, or an allowance, or whatever that sort of thing is to be called. Wherefore it is most foolish to say of temporal things that they ought to fail; since all such are so placed in this scheme of things that unless they fail the future cannot succeed the past, so that the whole of the beauty of times and seasons in their kind may be fulfilled. For in the measure that these things have received, they play their part, and in playing it make return to Him to whom they owe such being as they have. For he who laments that they should fail should take note of his own speech, of the very language of his complaint, to see if he thinks this to be fair and well-weighed. For considering only the sound of the words, if someone should fix his affections on one particular syllable, and not want it to fail and make place for those others, out of whose successive failing the

whole speech is made up, he would be judged marvellously
mad.

43.   In those things therefore which, because they have not received further being, fail in order that all things may be
accomplished in their times, no one may rightly blame their
failure; because no one can say: It ought to remain; since it
cannot go beyond the bounds it has received. But in rational
creatures, by whom, whether they sin or sin not, the beauty
of the universe finds its crowning glory, either there are no
sins—which is a silly thing to say, for he at any rate sins who
would condemn as sins things which are not sins—or sins
should not be blamed, which is no less absurd, for things not
rightly done will begin then to be praised, and the mind
will lose all sense of direction, and life will become chaos;
or a deed will be blamed for being done as it ought to be,
and a damnable madness, or to speak more mildly, a most
wretched error will arise. Or if truest reason compels us, as it
does compel us, both to blame sins and to blame whatever is
rightly blamed because it is not as it ought to be: seek what
it is that a sinful nature owes, and you will find right-doing;
seek him to whom it is owing, and you will find God. For
from Him from whom the nature received the power to do
rightly when it would, it received also that it should be unhappy if it should not do right, and happy if it should.

44.   For because no one is superior to the laws of the omni-
potent Creator, the soul is not permitted to evade the debt.
For it either repays by using rightly what it has received, or it
repays by losing what it has been unwilling to use rightly.
And so, if it does not repay by doing justice, it repays by
suffering [unhappiness], because in both expressions there is
an echo of that word debt. For we could also express it in
this way: If it does not repay by doing what it ought, it will
repay by suffering what it ought. These moreover are not
separated by any interval of time. So that one should not do
what he ought at one time, and suffer what he ought at
another, lest the universal beauty be defiled for a single in-

stant, so as to have the disgrace of sin without the grace of punishment. But whatever is now avenged in hidden ways is reserved for the judgment to come to be made manifest, and for the keenest sense of misery. For just as he who is not awake sleeps, so he who does not do what he should, suffers without an instant's pause what he should; since the happiness of justice is so great that no one can depart from it save to unhappiness. In all failures therefore either the things that fail have not received further being, and there is no fault, just as also while they are there is no fault, since it has not been given to them to be more than they are: or they have been unwilling to be that which it was given them to be if they so willed; and because this is a good, they stand accused for their unwillingness.

CHAPTER XVI

Our sins cannot be put back on God.

45.   God, however, owes nothing to anyone, because He supplies all things without recompense. And although someone may say that something is owing to him for his merits, yet surely it is not due him that he should be; he certainly is not the one to whom anything is owing. And after all, what merit is there in being turned to Him from whom you are, so that from Him from whom you have your being you may also be better? What then do you ask of Him that you may demand as something owing? For even if you were unwilling to turn to Him, He would lack nothing; whereas to you He is lacking without whom you would be nothing, and from whom you are such that unless you turn to Him, and give Him back the being that you have from Him, you will be not nothing, to be sure, but unhappy. All things therefore owe to Him first whatever they are, in so far as they are natures. Then those that have received the power to will owe to Him whatever better thing they can be if they will, and whatever they should be. No one stands accused therefore

because of that which he has not received; but because he has not done what was due from him he justly stands accused. He is a debtor, however, if he has received both free will and sufficient power.

46.   Altogether, therefore, when anyone does not do what is owing from him it is never a fault of the Creator, so that it is even to His glory that one suffers what he ought; and from the very fact that he is blamed for not doing as he ought, He only to whom you owe it is praised. For if you are praised for seeing what you ought to do, while you see it only in Him who is truth immutable, how much more is He praised, who commands you to will, and has bestowed the power, and does not permit your unwillingness to go unpunished?

For if everyone owes that which he has received, and man were so made that he sins by necessity, he owes it that he should sin. Therefore when he sins he does as he ought. But if this is a wicked thing to say, then no one is forced to sin by his own nature. But neither is he forced by another nature. For no one sins when he suffers aught that he would not. For if he suffers justly, he does not sin in that which he suffers against his will; but he has sinned in that which he has done willingly, so that he rightly suffers that which he would not. But if he suffers unjustly, how does he sin? For sin is not to suffer unjustly, but to do unjustly. But if one is forced to sin neither by his own nature nor by another nature, it remains that he sins by his own will. For if you would ascribe it to the Creator you acquit the sinner, who has then done nothing beyond the purposes of the Creator. But if he is rightly defended he has not sinned, so that there is nothing to ascribe to the Creator. If the sinner can be defended, let us then praise the Creator: let us praise Him if he cannot. For if he be justly defended, he is not a sinner: praise therefore the Creator. But if he cannot be defended, he is a sinner in the measure that he has turned away from the Creator: praise therefore the Creator.

I do not find at all therefore, and affirm that there cannot be found, and that there is absolutely no way in which our sins can be imputed to God our Creator; because I find that He is to be praised in those very sins, not only because He punishes them, but also because they are committed by turning away from His truth.

E. I accept and approve these things most gladly, and agree that it is altogether true that it can never happen that our sins are rightly to be ascribed to our Creator.

CHAPTER XVII

The will is the first cause of sinning.

47.   But I should nevertheless like to know, if that is possible, why that nature does not sin which God has foreknown would not sin, and why that other sins which He has foreknown would sin. For I do not now think that God's foreknowledge compels either the one to sin or the other to sin not. But if there were no reason for this, rational creatures would not be so divided that some would never sin, some would continue in sin, and some, as a sort of mean between these two, would sometimes sin and sometimes be turned to right action. What is the cause of this threefold distribution? But I do not want to be told: the will; for I am seeking the cause of the will itself. For there must be a reason why this one never wills to sin, that other never wills not, while a third sometimes wills and sometimes wills not; since all three are of the same genus. For all that seems clear to me is that this threefold character of the rational will must have a cause; but what that cause may be, I know not.

48. *A.* Since the will is the cause of sin, and you moreover are asking for the cause of the will itself—supposing I do find this, will you not then be wanting to know the cause also of the cause which I have found? And what manner of inquiry is that, and where will be the end of our investigating and discussing; whereas in fact you should want only to know the

root? Beware lest you think that anything truer can be said than what has been said: *The root of all evils is avarice,** that is, wanting more than enough. But that is enough which the measure of a nature needs to maintain itself in its own kind. For avarice, which in Greek is called *philargyria,* is not only in silver and coins, (though the word is probably derived from the fact that among the ancients coins were generally made of silver or silver alloy) but is to be understood as the immoderate desire of all things, whever in any way anyone wants more than enough. But this avarice is concupiscence, and concupiscence moreover is a depraved will. Therefore a depraved will is the cause of all evils. But if such a will were according to nature, it would certainly maintain that nature and would not be harmful to it, and hence would not be depraved. Whence it follows that the root of all evils is not according to nature; which is enough to oppose those who would indict natures. But if you demand a cause for this root, how then will it be the root of all evils? For that will be the root which is the cause of this; and when you have found it, as I said, you will be wanting to know the cause of that, and there will be no bounds to your questioning.

49.   But after all, what cause of the will could there be before the will itself? For it is either the will itself, and there is no going back of that root of the will; or it is not the will, and has no sin. Either, therefore, the will is the first cause of sinning, or no sin is the first cause of sinning. Nor is sin rightly imputed to anyone but a sinner. It is therefore not rightly imputed to him unless he is willing: but I do not know why you want to ask anything else. Finally, whatever be the cause of the will, it is certainly either just or unjust. If it is just, whoever obeys it will not sin. If it is unjust, let him not obey it, and he will not sin.

---

*I Tim., VI, 10.

CHAPTER XVIII

Whether anyone may sin in that which he cannot guard against.

50. Is it perhaps force, which compels one against his will? How many times will we have to repeat the same thing? Remember all those things which we said earlier about sin and free will. But if it is too much trouble to commit all those things to memory, take this, which is very short. Whatever is the cause of the will, if it cannot be resisted, it is no sin to yield to it; but if it can be resisted, one should not yield to it, and he will not sin. Does it perchance deceive the unwary? Then beware of deception. But is it so deceptive that it is quite impossible to be on one's guard? If that is so, there are no sins. For who sins in those things which he can in no way guard against? But men do sin. Therefore it is possible to guard against sin.

51. And yet even certain things done through ignorance are blamed and judged to need correcting, as we read in the Holy Scriptures; for the Apostle says: *I obtained mercy of God, because I acted in ignorance.** And the prophet says: *Remember not the sins of my youth and of my ignorance.* Even things done by necessity are to be blamed, when a man would do right, but cannot; for whence are these voices: *For the good that I would, I do not; but the evil that I would not, that I do.†* And this: *To will is present with me; but how to perform that which is good, I find not.‡* And this: *For the flesh lusteth against the spirit, and the spirit against the flesh. For these are contrary to one another, so that you do not the things you will.§* But all these things are characteristic of men coming from that damnation of death; for if it is not that punishment of man, but his nature, these things are not

---

*I Tim. I, 13.
†Romans, VII, 19.
‡Romans, VII, 18.
§Galatians, V, 17.

sins. For if he does not depart from that manner in which he was made by nature, so that it cannot be better, he does what he ought when he does these things. But if man would be good were he otherwise, but being what he now is, is not good, and does not have it in his power to be good—either because he cannot see what sort of man he ought to be, or because he sees and yet has not the strength to be as he sees he should be—who can doubt that this condition is a penalty? But every penalty, if it is just, is a penalty for sin, and is called punishment: but if it is an unjust penalty, since no one doubts that it is a penalty, it is imposed on man by some unjust ruler. But then, since only a madman could doubt the omnipotence and justice of God, this penalty is just, and is being paid for some sin. For no unjust ruler could steal man away from God without God's knowledge, or wrest him away against God's will—as if God were too weak, or to be bullied or frightened—in order to torture man by an unjust penalty. It follows therefore that this just penalty comes from man's damnation.

52.   Nor is it any wonder either that because of ignorance man has not a free judgment of will for choosing what he should rightly do; or that by the opposition of carnal habit, which by the force of the mortal succession has become a sort of second nature, man sees what he should rightly do, and wants to do it, but cannot accomplish it. For that is the most just penalty of sin: that each one loses that which he is unwilling to use rightly; when he could so use it without any difficulty if he were willing. For thus it is that whoever knowingly does what is not right, loses the power to know what is right; and whoever has been unwilling to do right when he could loses the power to do it when he would. For in fact these two, ignorance and difficulty, beset every sinful soul as penalties. Through ignorance it is disgraced by error; through difficulty it is tormented by pain. But the approving of false things as true, so as to err unwillingly, and the impotence to

refrain from carnal works, because of the resistance and the torment of the bonds of flesh, are not of the nature of man as originally created, but are penalties of man condemned. But when we speak of the free will to do right, we are speaking of that will with which man was made.

CHAPTER XIX

Sinners may not plead in excuse for their ignorance and diffi-culty the imperfection transmitted to them by the sin of Adam.

53.   Here comes up that question which grumbling men, who in their sinning are readier for anything rather than accuse themselves, are wont to bandy about. For they say: If Adam and Eve sinned, what have we miserable creatures done, that when born with the blindness of ignorance and the pains of difficulty, we should first err unwittingly as to what we should do, and then, when the precepts of justice begin to become clear and we should wish to follow them, we should not be able to do so because of the opposition of some necessity or other of carnal desire?

These should be told curtly to be quiet, and to stop mur-muring against God. Rightly, perhaps, would they complain, if there had arisen no conqueror of the errors and lusts of men. But when He is everywhere present, who through the creation that serves Him as Lord calls back those who have turned away from Him; who teaches the faithful, encourages the hopeful, exhorts the diligent, aids the struggling, and hearkens to them that pray to Him. That which you do not know in spite of your desire to know is not counted as your fault, but that which not knowing you neglect to seek. It is not that you do not bind up your wounded members; but that you think naught of Him that would heal you. Those sins are your very own. For from no man is taken the knowledge of how to seek profitably that which it is unprofitable not to know,[1] and that weakness should be humbly confessed, so that He who neither errs nor labors in His coming may come to the help of those who seek and confess.

54.   For that which one does wrongly because of ignorance, and that which one willing rightly yet cannot do are called sins for the reason that they have their origin in that sin of the free will, for that earlier sin has earned these as consequences. For just as we speak of a tongue, not only for the member that we move in the mouth when we speak, but also for what follows from the motion of this member, that is, the form and sequence of the words, so that with this meaning we speak of the Greek tongue, or the Latin tongue; so we call sins, not only those properly so called, committed with knowledge by a free will, but also those which must necessarily follow from the punishment of this sin. Similarly we speak of nature in one way when we speak properly of the nature of man as he was first created blameless in his own kind, and in another way to mean that nature in which we are born, condemned to the punishment of that first man, and mortal, and ignorant, and in bondage to the flesh; according to which manner the Apostle says: *For we also were by nature children of wrath, as were the rest.**

CHAPTER XX

Penal defects have descended not at all unjustly to the progeny of Adam, whatever may finally be the true opinion as to the origin of souls.

56.   But that from that first union we should be born with ignorance, and impotence, and mortality, because our first parents, when they sinned, were cast down into error, and hardship, and death, has most justly pleased God the supreme ruler of things; in order that in the birth of man should be

---

[1] For from no man is taken the knowledge that that is profitably sought which is unprofitably not known. M.

*Ephes. II, 3.

revealed the justice of Him Who punishes and in his progress toward salvation the mercy of Him who sets him free. For happiness was not so taken from the first man in his condemnation that he was also deprived of fecundity. For from his offspring, carnal and mortal though this was, could be made something that in its own kind would be an honor and ornament to the earth. But it did not accord with equity that he should beget offspring better than himself. But each ought to be not only not prohibited from turning to God if he would, so as to overcome the punishment which his origin had merited as the result of his turning away, but each ought even to be helped: for thus also the Creator showed how easily man could have retained, had he so willed, the nature in which he was made; when his progeny were able also to overcome what by nature it was born to be.

56.   For if one soul were created, and the souls of all other men generated from this at birth, who can say that they have not sinned when that first one has sinned? But if they are created one by one as each one is born, it is seen to be not perverse, but indeed most meet and just—ordered, that the demerit of the earlier should be the nature of those that followed, and that good desert in the later should be the nature of the earlier. For what is there unworthy if the Creator wished even to show that the dignity of the soul so far excelled that of corporeal creatures that one could arise from that level to which the fall of another had brought him? For when that first sinful soul comes to ignorance and hardship, it is rightly called a penalty, because it was better before this penalty. If then that other began, not only before all sinning, but before all its life, to be such as the first had been after its life had become culpable, it has no small good for which to thank its Creator; because its very birth and beginning is better than the most perfect body. For these are not trifling goods, not only that the soul should be of a nature that is already superior to any body, but also that with

the help of its Creator it has the faculty to ennoble itself, and by pious zeal acquire and lay hold on all virtues, through which it is freed from torturing hardship and blinding ignorance. If this is the case, ignorance and hardship will be for souls at birth not a punishment for sin, but an admonition to progress, and the beginning of perfection. For it is no little thing that the soul, before all desert of good works, should have received a natural discernment by which it places wisdom above error, and peace above difficulty; so that it comes to these, not by being born, but by its efforts. If it shall have been unwilling to do this it will rightly be held guilty of sin, as one which has not used well the power which it has received. For though born in ignorance and difficulty, it was not constrained by any necessity to continue as it was born. And no one indeed but almighty God could be the creator of such souls, which He made even when not loved, and which loving them He remakes, and when they love Him, makes perfect; who when they did not exist was responsible for their being; and for their happiness when they love Him from whom they are.

57.   But if from some secret place souls now existing are sent by God to animate and rule the bodies of each one as he is born, they are surely sent with this duty: to rule well the body born with the penalty of sin, the mortality of the first man; that is, by purifying it by virtues, and subjecting it to a well ordered and lawful servitude, to prepare even for it at the proper time and order a place of heavenly incorruption. Which souls, when they enter into this life, and take on the management of a mortal frame, must needs take on also both oblivion of their former life and the labor of the present one: whence follow that ignorance and hardship which were in the first man the punishment of mortality to pay for the soul's wretchedness; but which in these is a door to the service of regaining incorruption of the body. For in this case too these are not called sins, except that the flesh coming from the

offspring of a sinner makes the ignorance and hardship for souls coming to it; which ignorance and hardship can be counted as faults neither to these souls nor to their Creator. For He gave both the power to work well at laborious tasks, and the way of faith in the blindness of oblivion; and especially that discernment by which every soul realizes that it should seek to know what it is unprofitable to be ignorant of, and should work unceasingly at arduous tasks so as to overcome the difficulty of doing right, and should implore the Creator to aid the struggling with His might: that Creator who either outwardly by His law, or by his speaking in the secret hearts of men, commands them to endeavor, and who prepares the glory of His most blessed city for those who triumph over him who by his wicked suasion overcame the first man and brought him to his miserable state; which miserable state they take upon themselves that they may vanquish him by their most excellent faith. For it is a battle of no small glory, to overcome the devil by taking upon oneself the same punishment by which he boasts of bringing upon the man he overcame. But whoever, held in thrall by his love of this life, shall have neglected to do this, will in no way ascribe the shame of his desertion to the rule of his King, but under the Lord of all will be ordered within the region of him whose shameful pay he loved so well as to desert his own camp.

58.   But if, again, souls stationed elsewhere are not sent by the Lord God, but come of their own accord to dwell in bodies, it is easy to see then that any ignorance and difficulty that pursued them was of their own choosing, and hence the Creator is in no way to be blamed for it; because even if He himself had sent them, He also, in that very ignorance and difficulty, did not deprive them of their free will to seek and inquire and endeavor, and would give to those that sought, and show to those that inquired, and open to those that knocked; and so was altogether without fault. For he would hold out this ignorance and difficulty to the zealous and well-

wishing to be overcome, and to avail as a crown of glory; but to those neglecting, and wishing to excuse their sins on account of weakness, He would not put ignorance and difficulty itself in their way for their accusation; but because they willed to continue in them, rather than by zeal of inquiry and learning, and humility of confession and prayer, to arrive at truth and peace, He would visit them with a just punishment.

CHAPTER XXI

A pernicious error in the foregoing matter.

59.   But as to these four opinions concerning the soul, no one should be rash enough to make an affirmation whether souls come by propagation, or are made new in each one as he is born, or are already existing somewhere and are sent into bodies coming to birth, or slip into bodies of their own accord. For either the question has not yet been expounded and elucidated by Catholic commentators on the sacred Books, as fully as its obscurity and perplexity deserves, or if this has been done, such writings have not yet come into our hands. May our faith be sufficient to keep us from holding any false or unworthy opinion concerning the substance of the Creator; for we make our way toward Him by the road of piety. If therefore we think of Him otherwise than as He is, our efforts drive us not toward happiness, but toward emptiness. But if we hold any opinion concerning creation that is not in accord with fact, so long as we do not hold it as clearly known there is no danger. For we are not commanded to go to creation to be made happy, but to the Creator himself; concerning whom if we are persuaded of anything other than as things should be and are, we are deceived by most pernicious error. For by progress toward that which either does not exist, or if it does, does not make men happy, no one can attain a happy life.

60.   But for the contemplation of the eternity of truth, so as to be able to rejoice in it and cleave to it, a path away from

temporal things is prepared for our infirmity, in order that we may believe so much about things past and to come as suffices for the journey of those proceeding to things eternal. This discipline of the faith is governed by divine mercy, so that its authority is very great. But things of the present, which concern the creature in the mobility and mutability of his body and mind, are perceived as transient. In these we cannot hold in any sort of knowledge anything that we do not experience. Whatever things, therefore, are told us by divine authority about created things, whether past or future, are to be believed; although some of these have passed before we could have witnessed them, and some have not yet reached our senses. Nevertheless, they are to be belived undoubtingly, because they have great power to strengthen our hope and to encourage our love, while they show us, through their ordered sequence of events, how God does not neglect our deliverance. But any error that assumes the guise of divine authority is refuted chiefly by this reasoning: it is proved to believe or affirm either that there is some mutable species apart from God's creation, or that there is some mutable species in God's substance, or else it contends that the substance of God is either more or less than the Trinity. To understand this Trinity with piety and reverence all Christian vigilance should be alert, and all its progress should be directed to this. But of the unity and equality of this Trinity, and of the particular attributes of each of the persons in it, this is not the place to treat. For to speak concerning the Lord God, author, and fashioner, and disposer of all things, about some things that pertain to the most wholesome faith, and by which the suckling intention, just beginning to raise itself from earthly matter toward heavenly, is aided and supported, is easy to do and has been done repeatedly by many. But to treat the whole matter thoroughly, and so present it that every human understanding, as far as may be in this life, may subject it to clear reason, is beyond the powers, not only of expression, but

of thought for any man; or at least for us does not seem
sufficiently clear and easy of approach.

So let us then complete what we have begun, so far as we
are aided and permitted. Whatever, regarding Creation, is
narrated to us as things past, or foretold as things to come,
which serves to give into our keeping an intact religion, or to
arouse us to a most sincere love of God and of our neighbor,
is to be believed without doubt. Against unbelievers, moreover, such things are so far to be defended that either their
unbelief is crushed by the weight of authority, or it is shown
to them, as far as may be, first how it is not foolish to believe
such things, and then how foolish it is not to believe them.
However, false doctrine should be refuted not so much by
things past and future as by things present, and chiefly by
immutable things, and as far as is permitted overcome by
clear reasoning.

61.   But indeed, in the sequence of things temporal, the expec-
tation of things to come is to be preferred to inquiry as to
things past. For even in Holy Scripture those past events
which are narrated bear before themselves either a prefigur-
ing, or a promise, or a testimony of things to come. And in
truth, even in those things prosperous and adverse, which
pertain to this life, what anyone may have been is not very
important, but all care and worry is centered on what is hoped
will be. By some intimate and natural instinct or other, those
things which have befallen us, being over and done with, are
to us at a moment of happiness or misery as if they had never
happened. What harm then is it to me if I do not know when
I began to be, since I know that I am, and do not despair of
future existance? For I do not so attend to past things that
I fear some harmful error if I have thought of those things
otherwise than as they were; but, led by the mercy of God my
maker, direct my course to that which I am going to be. Concerning, therefore, what I am to be, and concerning Him with
whom I am going to be, to think or believe otherwise than

as it is in truth is an error which I must vigorously beware of, lest mistaking one thing for another I should not provide myself with needed things, or should not be able to reach the end I have set myself. For just as there would be nothing to hinder my procuring clothing if I had forgotten the past winter, whereas I should be hindered if I did not believe that future cold threatens; so it will be no hindrance to my soul if perchance it has forgotten what it has experienced, if only it diligently turns toward and holds to what it is admonished to prepare itself for hereafter. Just as, for example, it would do no harm to one sailing for Rome to forget entirely from what shore he had set sail, if notwithstanding he were not ignorant of how to set his course from where he happened to be, whereas it would do him no good to remember the coast from which he had started, if having a false notion of the port of Rome he should run upon a rock: so, even if I have not known the beginning of the time of my life, it will be no harm to me knowing in what end I shall rest; nor would any recollection or conjecture about the beginning of life profit me, if thinking other than worthily about God, who is the sole end of the soul's labors, I should run upon the rocks of error.

62.   Nor is this discourse intended to make anyone think that we forbid those who can do so from seeking according to the divinely inspired Scriptures, whether soul is propagated from soul, or whether they are made singly to animate each one, or whether they are sent from somewhere by divine command to rule and animate the body, or whether they insinuate themselves of their own volition; if reason demands the consideration of these matters for the clearing up of some necessary problem, or if leisure is granted from the discussion of any inquiry into more necessary matters. But I would say this about the question: that one should in such a matter not be hasty in his anger at another who with a doubt that is only human does not yield to his opinion; or even if someone

understands these things surely and clearly, should he on that account think that another has forfeited hope of things to come, because he does not call to mind the beginning of things past.

CHAPTER XXII

If ignorance and difficulty are natural to man, our reasons for praising the Creator are not thereby lacking.

63.   However things may stand in this matter, whether it should be passed over altogether, or postponed for later consideration, the present question is not hindered from showing clearly that by the most pure and just and unshaken and immutable majesty and substance of the Creator, the souls of sinners pay the penalty for their sins; which sins, as has already been argued at length, are to be attributed to the sinner's will alone, and no further cause is to be sought.

64.   But if ignorance and difficulty are natural, the soul begins its journey from them, and moves forward to knowledge and repose [until the happy life be perfected in it]. If of its own will it neglects thus to set out with piety and with its best endeavors, the capacity for which is not denied it, it is justly plunged into greater ignorance and difficulty, which now is penal, and by a most meet and seemly disposition of affairs ordered among inferior things. For the soul is not held to account for not knowing or doing what by nature it does not know and cannot do, but for not having striven to know, and for not laboring worthily to acquire ease in well-doing. For not to know how to speak, and not to be able to, is natural to an infant; which ignorance and difficulty of speech are not only blameless under the laws of grammarians, but are even sweet and pleasing to human affections; for the child did not by any fault neglect to acquire this faculty, or by any fault lose what it had acquired. And so, if happiness were based for us on eloquence, and it were so held in reproach to sin in pronunciation, in the same way as when we sin in the acts of

life, no one surely would be blamed for infancy because he had arisen out of it to pursue eloquence, but clearly he would be deservedly blamed, if by the perversity of his own will he had fallen back to it, or had remained in it. So too now, if ignorance of the truth and difficulty of doing right are natural to man, and he begins from these his rise to the happiness of wisdom and repose, no one rightly blames these for their natural beginnings. But if he is unwilling to set forth, or is willing to slip back after he has set forth, he will pay penalties rightly and deservedly.

65. His Creator, however, is in all respects to be praised; either because He implanted in the soul from those very beginnings a capacity for the supreme good, or because He aids man in his progress, or because He satisfies and makes perfect him who goes forward, or because He sets in order the sinner —that is for him who either refuses to raise himself to perfection from his beginnings, or falls back from some progress already made by a most just damnation according to his deserts. For He did not thereby make the soul evil because it is not yet as great as it can become by progress; since from its beginning all perfections of bodies are far inferior to it, and these are yet judged laudable in their own kind by anyone who judges soundly. That the soul is ignorant of what it should do, is because it has not yet received knowledge; but it will receive this also if it uses well the power it has received. For it has received the power to seek reverently and diligently if it will. And that knowing what it should do, it has not the power to accomplish it forthwith, this too it has not received. For a certain higher part of it has gone ahead to perceive the good that should rightly be done, but a certain laggard and carnal part is not consequently carried along in this perception; so that from this difficulty it is admonished to call to the helper of its perfection, whom it perceives to be the author of its beginning, that He may thereby become dearer to the soul, while not by its own

powers, but by those of Him by whose mercy it has its being, it is raised to beatitude. But the more dear it is to Him from whom it is, the more immoveable does it rest in Him, and the more aboundingly does it enjoy His eternity. For if a young, new-planted slip of a tree can nowise rightly be called sterile, though it may have passed several summers without fruit, until at due season it will come to bear; why should not the Author of the soul be praised with due piety for giving it such a beginning that by its own endeavors and progress it may attain to the fruit of wisdom and justice, and for giving it such dignity that He has even placed it in its power to go on, if it will, to beatitude?

CHAPTER XXIII

The complaint of ignorant men about the death of little children, and about the bodily torments with which they are afflicted, is unjust. What pain is.

66.   But to this argument a certain carping objection is wont to be made by ignorant people, regarding the death of infants, and some of the bodily sufferings with which we often see them afflicted. For they say: What need was there that he should be born, who before he could enter upon any merit of life has departed from life? Or what will be the future judgment regarding him for whom there is no place among the just, for he has done nothing rightly; nor among the wicked, for he has never sinned?[1]

To such it is answered: In the breadth of the universe, and in the ordered connection of all creation throughout space and time, no man whatsoever can be created superfluously, where no leaf on a tree is created superfluously; but it is surely superfluous to inquire concerning the deserts of him who has deserved nothing. For it is not to be feared that there could

---

[1] Or to what class will he be assigned in the future judgment for whom there is no place among the just, for he has done nothing rightly; nor among the wicked, for he has never sinned? M.

be a life which is a mean between righteousness and sin, and no sentence of the judge intermediate between reward and punishment.

67.   At this point men are wont to raise that other question, as to what good the sacrament of the baptism of Christ is to infants, who after receiving it frequently die before they have been able to know anything about it. In which matter it is enough that it is piously and rightly believed that the faith of those who bring the child to be baptized is of advantage to the child. And this too is commended by the most wholesome authority of the Church, so that from it each one may perceive how much his own faith benefits him, when to the benefit of others, who have as yet no faith of their own, the faith of others can be adapted. For what advantage to the son of the widow was his own faith, which he certainly did not have when he was dead; while his mother's faith availed to raise him again? How much more, therefore, can the faith of another benefit the child to whom his own lack of faith cannot be imputed?

69.   Concerning the bodily sufferings moreover which afflict small children, who have done no sin by reason of their age (unless the souls which animate them have sinned before they began to be human), a great lament, and as it were a tender-hearted one, is set up when it is said: What evil have they done that they should suffer these things? As if there could be merit of innocence before one could harm anything. But since God works some good in correcting the parents, when they are scourged by the sufferings and deaths of the little ones who are dear to them, why should not these things be done, when after they have passed they will be as if they had never happened in those in whom they were done? Those for whose sake they were done will either be better, if chastened by temporal trials they elect to live more uprightly; or they will have no excuse in the punishment of the final judgment, if with the distress of this life they shall be unwilling

to turn their desire toward the life eternal. Who knows moreover how far faith is exercised or mercy is tested by these little ones, by whose suffering the hardness of the parents is broken: who then knows what good compensation God may reserve, in the secrecy of His judgments, for these same little ones, who although they have done nothing rightly, have nevertheless suffered these things when they have done no sin? For not without reason does the Church commend to us those children who were slain by Herod, when he sought out our Lord Jesus Christ to slay Him, and who are received into the honor of Martyrs.

69.   However, these artful critics, and those who are not very careful examiners of such questions, but most loquacious airers of them, are wont to trouble the faith of the less learned even over the sufferings and hardships of animals, saying: What have the beasts either deserved of ill that they should suffer such hardships, or what good may they hope for that they should be tried by them? But they say or think these things because they judge of things most unfairly, who being incapable of perceiving what and how great is the supreme good, would have all things such as they think the supreme good to be. For they cannot conceive of a supreme good above the highest bodies, which are celestial and less subject to corruption; and they therefore demand, with no regard for order, that the bodies of animals shall not suffer death or any corruption, as if, though lowest, they were not mortal; or they think them bad because celestial bodies are better.

But the pain which animals feel shows us a certain animal force in the soul which is in its own kind wonderful and praiseworthy. For from this very thing it is quite clear by the way they rule and animate their bodies how they are in quest of unity. For what else is pain but a certain sense that is impatient of division or corruption? Whence it is clearer than light how that soul in the whole of its body is eager for and tenacious of unity, which neither willingly nor indifferently, but rather with struggle and opposition, is excited to that suffering of its body by which it refuses to accept that its unity and integrity be shaken. Were it not for the sufferings of animals, it would not be clear to us how great this craving for unity is in lower living creatures. If this were not clear to us we might be insufficiently reminded that all these creatures were constituted by that supreme and sublime and ineffable unity of the Creator.

70.   And in truth, if you hearken reverently and attentively, every appearance and movement of created nature which falls within our ken, by its diverse movements and affections utters a lesson for us, as by a variety of tongues; calling out and shouting to us that the Creator must be acknowledged. For of those things that feel neither pain nor pleasure, there is not one that does not by some unity attain to the beauty of its kind, or wholly to whatever sort of stability belongs to its nature. Likewise, of those creatures that feel the hurt of pain or the delight of pleasure, there is not one that does not acknowledge, by the very fact that it flees pain and seeks pleasure, that it flees disintegration and seeks unity. And in rational souls themselves, all the seeking for knowledge in which the rational nature takes its joy both reduces to unity everything which it perceives, and in avoiding error is only fleeing from the confusion of incomprehensible ambiguity. But why is every ambiguity vexatious, except that it has not an assured unity? From this it is clear that all things, whether they offend or are offended, whether they delight or are delighted, intimate and proclaim the unity of the Creator. But if ignorance and difficulty, from which this life must needs begin, are not natural to souls, it follows that they have been taken up as a duty, or imposed as a punishment. Concerning which I think we have had enough discussion.

CHAPTER XXIV

*The first man was not made foolish, but capable of wisdom.
What folly is.*

71.   Wherefore it is more important to inquire what kind of
man was first made, than as to how his posterity was propagated. For they think they are proposing a very shrewd question, who ask: If the first man was made wise, why was· he
led astray? But if he was made foolish, how is God not the
author of faults, since folly is a very great fault? As if, forsooth, the nature of man could not receive some intermediate
quality, [besides folly and wisdom], which could be called ·
neither folly nor wisdom. In that case a man begins to be
either foolish or wise, so as necessarily to be called one or
the other, when he could have wisdom if he did not so
neglect it that his will should be guilty of vicious folly. For
no one is so silly as to call an infant a fool, though he might
be yet sillier if he wanted to call it wise. Since, therefore, an
infant cannot be called either foolish or wise, although he is
already a man; it is clear from this that the nature of man
receives some middle quality which cannot rightly be called
either folly or wisdom. [So, also, if any one were animated
by such an affection as they have who through negligence lack
wisdom, no man would rightly call him foolish whom he
saw to be such by no vicious ignorance but by nature.] For
folly is not any kind of ignorance of what things to seek and
what to shun, but a wicked ignorance. For this reason we do
not call a dumb animal foolish, because it has not received
the power to be wise. Neverthless, we often do give a name
to a thing improperly, by analogy. For while blindness is also
a very great fault of the eyes, it is nevertheless not a fault
in new-born kittens, and cannot properly be called blindness.

72.   If therefore man was so made, that although not yet wise,
he could neverthless receive a command which he ought
certainly to obey, it is neither wonderful that he could be led
astray, nor unjust that he should pay penalties for not obey-

ing the command. Nor is the Creator the author of his faults; because not to have wisdom was not yet a fault of man, if he had not yet been given the power to have it. But he had nevertheless been given that by which, if he chose to use it well, he could ascend to what he did not yet possess. For it is one thing to be rational, and another to be wise. By reason one becomes capable of receiving a command to which he owes fidelity, so that he does what is commanded. But just as he receives the command by the nature of reason, so he receives wisdom by obedience to the command.[1] For what nature is to the receiving of the command, the will is to the obedience of it. And just as a rational nature is, as it were, the merit receiving a command, so obedience to the command is the merit of receiving wisdom. But from the time a man begins to be capable of receiving a command, from that moment he begins to be able to sin. There are two ways, moreover, in which he sins before he becomes wise: if he does not fit himself to receive a command, or if having received it he does not obey it. But the wise man sins if he shall have turned himself away from wisdom. For just as a command is not from him who is commanded, but from him who commands; so also wisdom is not from him who is enlightened, but from him who gives the light. What is there then, for which glory should not be given to the Creator of man? For man is something good; and better than the beasts in that he is capable of being instructed. And better than this, when he receives the precept. Better again than this when he obeys the precept. And better than all of these, when he is blessed by the eternal light of wisdom.

But sin is evil in the negligence either to receive the precept, or to obey it, or to keep the contemplation of wisdom. From this it may be seen that even if the first man was made wise, he could still have been led astray. Which sin,

---

[1] But just as the nature of reason receives the command, so observance of the command receives wisdom. M.

being by his free choice, was by a just, divine law followed by punishment. For so says also the Apostle Paul: *Professing themselves to be wise, they become fools.** For pride turns away from wisdom, but the turning away brings folly. Folly is indeed a sort of blindness, just as the same Apostle says: *And their foolish heart was darkened.** But whence is this darkness, but from turning away from the light of wisdom? But whence this turning away, but that he to whom God is the final good would be to himself his own good, just as God is to Himself? And so, *To myself,* he says, *my soul is troubled.*† And then: *Taste, and you shall be as gods.*‡

73.   But thoughtful people are disturbed by a question which they put thus: Did the first man depart from God because of folly, or did he become foolish by departing? Because if you answer that it was because of folly that he departed from wisdom, it would seem that he was foolish before he departed from wisdom, so that that folly would be the cause of his departing. Again, if you answer that he became foolish by departing from wisdom, they ask whether he did foolishly or wisely in departing. For if he did wisely, he did rightly, and sinned not: if foolishly, then, say they, he was already in that folly which made him depart. For he could not do anything foolishly without folly. From this it is clear that there is a middle thing, by which one passes from wisdom to folly, which can be called neither a wise nor a foolish act, a thing which is given to be understood only in terms of opposites by men placed in this life. For no one among mortal men becomes wise without passing from folly to wisdom. But if the passage is done foolishly, it is assuredly not done well, which is a silly thing to say; but if it was done wisely, then there was wisdom in the man before he became wise, which is just as silly. From this we see that the passage is something intermediate which can be called neither. So too that the

---

*Romans, I, 22, 21.
†Psalm XLII, 6.
‡Gen. III, 5.

first man should pass over from the stronghold of wisdom to folly, that passing was neither foolish nor wise. It is just as with sleeping and waking: to sleep is not to be going to sleep, nor is waking up the same as being awake, but there is a sort of transition from one to the other. But there is this difference, that these are generally done without our willing them, whereas those others are never done except by willing, and hence are followed by just retributions.

CHAPTER XXV

By what things seem the rational nature is touched when it turns its intention to evil.

74.   But because the will is not invited to do anything unless something is seen, what each may accept or reject is in one's power; but there is no power over what is presented to view. It must be acknowledged that the mind is reached by the sight of things both higher and lower, so that it takes what it will from each; and from the desert of its taking either misery or happiness results. Just as in Eden, we have the admonition of God seen from higher things, and from lower the suggestion of the serpent. For neither what God commanded nor what the serpent suggested was in man's power. But how free that man is, untrammeled by any difficulty and constituted in the very health of wisdom, not to yield to the allurement of lower things which he sees, may be understood from this; that even the foolish overcome these things in order to pass over to wisdom, even with the vexation of foregoing the noxious sweetness of pernicious habits.

75.   But it may be asked at this point: If man had before him the sight of alternative things: the one the precept of God, and the other from the suggestion of the serpent, whence to the devil himself was suggested that design of pursuing impiety by which he fell from the seats of those on high? For if he were reached by nothing seen, he would not choose to do what he did; for if something had not come into his

mind he would in no wise have turned his course to wickedness. Whence then came that into his mind, whatever it was that did come, that made him endeavor to do those things by which he became the devil instead of a good angel? For whoever wills, surely wills to do something; and unless this is suggested to him from without by his bodily senses, or comes in secret ways into the mind, he cannot will. There are therefore to be distinguished two kinds of things seen, of which one has its origin in the will of someone who persuades, such as the devil, by consenting to whom man sinned; the other from things subject to the attention of the mind, or to the bodily senses. Everything is subject to the attention of the mind, except the immutable Trinity, which is indeed not subject, but rather is over it: subject therefore [to the intention of the mind] are first, the mind itself, by which too we perceive that we live; then the body which it rules, so that it moves it as the need arises for the performance of bodily functions. But to the senses are subject all bodies whatsoever.

76.   But as in the contemplation of Supreme Wisdom (which is certainly not the mind, for it is immutable) the mind, which is mutable, may also look upon itself, and in a certain way come into its own mental process. This can be done only with the difference by which it is not what God is, and yet is something which after God can seem good. But it is better when it forgets itself before the love of the immutable God, or utterly despises itself in comparison to Him. But if facing itself, as it were, it takes pleasure in imitating God wrongly, and wishes to enjoy its own power, it becomes less in the measure that it desires to be greater. And this is: *Pride is the beginning of sin, and the beginning of pride is man's apostasy from God.** But to the pride of the devil is added the most malevolent ill will, so that he persuaded man to this same pride by which he perceived himself to have been damned. Whence it happens that punishment should over-

---

*Ecclesiasticus, X, 13, 12.

take man to amend, rather than to kill him, so that to him to whom the devil had offered himself for the imitation of his pride, our Lord offered Himself for the imitation of His humility, through Whom we are promised eternal life; so that the blood of Christ being first paid for us, after ineffable labors and sufferings, we may cling to our Deliverer with so great a love, and so transported by His radiance, that no lower things we may see can wrest from us that higher vision; although even if something should suggest itself to our attention through our baser appetites, the everlasting damnation and torments of the devil should recall us.

77. But so great is the beauty of justice, so great the joy of the light eternal, that is, of the immutable Truth and Wisdom, that even if we were not permitted to remain in it for more than the space of one day, for this alone years innumerable of this life, full of delights and abundance of temporal goods, would rightly and deservedly be despised. For not with feigned or slight affection was it said: *For one day in thy courts is better than thousands.** Although also, in another sense, this may be taken so that thousands of days are made to signify mutability of time, whereas the immutable eternity is called by the name of one day.

I do not know that I have passed by anything that is wanting in answer to your questions, so far as God has deigned to vouchsafe it: although even if something occurs to you, the measure of the book compels us to make an end, and to rest at last from this discussion.

---

*Psalm LXXXIV, 10.

www.ingramcontent.com/pod-product-compliance
Lightning Source LLC
Chambersburg PA
CBHW032000040426
42448CB00006B/440